new perspectives

AN ENGLISH COURSE

Angela Bell and Hugh Knight

Oxford University Press 1987

© Oxford University Press 1987

Oxford University Press, Walton Street, Oxford OX2 6DP

Oxford New York Toronto
Delhi Bombay Calcutta Madras Karachi
Petaling Jaya Singapore Hong Kong Tokyo
Nairobi Dar es Salaam Cape Town
Melbourne Auckland

and associated companies in
Beirut Berlin Ibadan Mexico City Nicosia

Oxford is a trade mark of Oxford University Press

ISBN 0 19 831154 0

Typesetting by Oxford Publishing Services
Printed in Hong Kong.

Acknowledgements

Peggy Appiah: 'How the leopard got its spots' from *Tales of an Ashanti Father*. Reprinted by permission of Andre Deutsch Ltd.   John R. Bailey, Kenneth McLeish, David Spearman: 'The Garden of Eden' from *Gods and Men*. © John R. Bailey, Kenneth McLeish, David Spearman 1981. Reprinted by permission of Oxford University Press.   Ulli Beier: 'The Revolt Against God' from *The Origin of Life and Death*. Copyright Editions Buchet/Chantel, Paris. Reprinted with permission; 'Leopard' and 'Elephant' from *Yoruba Poetry*. Reprinted by permission of Cambridge University Press.   Alan Brownjohn: 'We are going to see the rabbit . . .' from *Collected Poems 1952–83*. Reprinted by permission of Martin Secker & Warburg Ltd.   Bani Roy Choudry: 'The Ramayana' from *The Story of Ramayana*. Reprinted by kind permission of Hemkunt Press, New Delhi-110028.   Walter de la Mare: extract from *The Listeners*. The Literary Trustees of Walter de la Mare and The Society of Authors and their representatives. Reprinted by permission.   Jean D'Costa: extract from *The Devils of Rose Hall*. Reprinted by permission of Longman Group Ltd.   Alan Garner: 'The Legend of Alderley' from *The Weirdstone of Brisingamen* © Alan Garner 1960, published by Collins. Reprinted by permission.   Nicolas Guillen: 'Sensemaya: A chant for killing a Snake' trans. by G.R. Coulthard. Reprinted by permission of Mrs. H. Coulthard.   Minji Karibo: extract from *Nigerian Student Verse 1959* selected by M. Banham. (Ibadan University 1960).   Jan Knappert: 'Abu Nuwasi and the two thieves' from Myths and Legends of *the Swahili* (1970). Reprinted by permission of the author.   Ann McGovern: 'The story of Harriet Tubman' adapted from *Runaway Slave*. Copyright © 1965 by Ann McGovern. Reprinted by permission of Scholastic Inc.   John Mbiti: 'Snake Song' from *Noah's Ark* by M. Harrison and C. Stuart Clark. (OUP 1983). Reprinted by permission of the author.   R.K. Narayan: 'Lost at Night' from *Swami and Friends*. Reprinted by permission of David Higham Associates Ltd.   Alma Norman: 'The Curse of Rose Hall' from *New Ships* ed. D.G. Wilson. (OUP 1975).   Ngumbu Njururi 'The Story of Sun and Moon' from *Agikuyu Folk Tales* (OUP 1966). Reprinted by permission of the author.   R.W. Reeves: 'In the beginning' and 'The Boomerang' from *The Legend of Moonie Jarl*. (Jacaranda Wiley Ltd 1964).   Theodore Roethke: 'The Meadow Mouse' from *The Collected Poems of Theodore Roethke*. Reprinted by permission of Faber and Faber Ltd.   Michael Rosen: 'I'm alone in the evening' from *Mind Your Own Business*. Reprinted by permission of Andre Deutsch Ltd.   Idries Shah: 'Back to Front' from *Caravan of Dreams* p.30. Reprinted by permission of Octagon Press Ltd.   Bani Singh: extract from *The Indian Storybook*. Reprinted by permission of William Heinemann Ltd.   Lil Smith: extract from *The Good Old Bad Old Days*. Reprinted by permission of Centerprise Trust Ltd.   Richard Wright: extract from *Black Boy (1970)*. Reprinted by permission of John Farquharson Ltd.

Every effort has been made to trace and contact copyright holders but this has not always been possible. We apologise for any infringement of copyright.

The publishers would like to thank the following for permission to reproduce photographs:

Alan Band Associates p.46 (bottom right); Bibliothèque Publique de Dijon p.94 (bottom); Bodleian Library, Oxford pp.94 (top), 95 (left and right); Bruce Coleman Ltd; pp.40–41 (all), 42 (both), 46 (bottom left), 47; Farmers Weekly p.46 (centre right); Richard and Sally Greenhill pp.4 (top, centre, right centre, left centre); Guide Dogs for the Blind Association p.46 (centre right); Eric and David Hosking p.46 (centre left); Rob Judges pp.4 (bottom left and right), 12 (all), 15 (all), 43 (all), 70; Frank Lane p.46 (top left); Network p.4 (top right).

The illustrations are by Oena Armstrong, Michael Beach, Andrew Brown, Derek Collard, Paul Finn, Roger Gorringe, Nick Harris, Clare Hatcher. Jonathan Heap, Sue Heap, Peter Joyce, Vanessa Luff, Alan Marks, Hugh Marshall, Ian Miller, David Parkins, Colin Rispin, Jeroo Roy, Susan Scott, Nich Sharratt, Lee Stannard, Duncan Storr, Barrie Thorpe, Martin White, Shaun Williams, Farida Zaman.

The cover illustration is by Christina Balit.

The authors would like to thank all the pupils who contributed their writing; the teachers and pupils of South Kilburn Community School, Willesden High School and William Gladstone High School who helped develop the material in this book; and Mary Worrall who helped and encouraged us at all stages.

Contents

Introduction: Stories   4

Reference Section
    The Stages of Writing   12
    Getting it Right   18

Themes and Stories
1   Creation   22
2   The Story of Sun and Moon   33
3   Animals   40
4   Stories from the Ramayana   50
5   The Story of Harriet Tubman   58
6   Fears and Superstitions   66
7   The Canterbury Tales   80

Stories

Contents

Telling Stories
  The Good Old Bad Old Days
  Stories You Know
  Back to Front

Retelling Stories
  Abu Nuwasi and the Two Thieves
  Ways of Retelling Stories
  The Legend of Alderley

Your Writing
  The Stages of Writing

Other things to do
  Presenting your work
  Writing
  Reading

Telling Stories

Everyone knows lots of stories.
They tell jokes.
They gossip.
They remember funny or exciting
things that happened to them
when they were younger.

They tell each other
what happened in TV
programmes.
They read favourite books or tell favourite stories over
and over again.
They read stories in the newspaper, or watch and
listen to people telling what happened to them on
television and radio.
And if a few people are doing something new or
difficult together, there's always one person who's
ready with a story to scare the others:

I remember a
film once, when
these kids were
walking home late
at night, and
suddenly
....
......

I read about
a school somewhere,
and do you know what
they did to the first
years? Well, first
of all, they....

Even an ordinary event can make a good story, if it's told in a way that the reader will enjoy — like this story told by Lil Smith about a Saturday night in her childhood sixty years ago.

The Good Old Bad Old Days

Saturday night was bath night, which I hated. Not because I hated a bath, but it was the way it had to be done. It was such a small kitchen that the bath was hanging up on a nail out in the yard — a tin bath. But it was such a small kitchen that it wouldn't go on the floor between the fireplace and the table. So it had to go on the table. And next door's kitchen overlooked our kitchen, and they could see us all having our bath, which I did not like. Now we started with Phyllis who was the luckiest of all because she had clean water and the only two clean towels we had. Mum used to have the big iron saucepans on top of the hob, getting hotter all the time. My job was to dry them as they came out. We went in numbers, Phyllis first. It was very hard to dry Phyllis as she was partially paralysed and used to have a very bad temper. We had no nighties or pyjamas. We put our clean vest on and went and sat on the bed in the back room, because this was the night when we had a cup of cocoa, the only night of the week. Next comes Jacky, who was always as black as your hat. And the water is now getting slightly discoloured. Also another saucepan of water goes in — hot water — and the towels are getting a bit damp. I dry Jacky, and so forth, till it gets to Charlie. Now, by this

time, the two towels are soaking wet. So Charlie has to dry himself on the others' dirty under-clothes.

Now comes ME. I kick up a stink because I don't want to stand on the table because the Wrights next door could see me. I used to get a wallop on my bare behind for a start. Another saucepan of water would go in and I now got in to a pale grey soup. I had to wash my hair, which was very long, in this. We all had to wash our hair in this. And eventually I had two wet towels, every-body's wet underclothes, and my own dry under-clothes, to dry on.

Lil Smith

Stories You Know

Try telling some stories to a friend, or to the class. Tape-recording the best stories will help you to remember them, and the way they were told.

These questions will help you to think of some stories.

1 What's the oldest funny story you know?
2 What's the most important, exciting or memorable thing that ever happened to you?
3 What's the best programme with a story you've watched on TV recently?
4 Which story do you remember best from when you were young?
5 Are there any stories you would like to read, listen to or watch on film or television again?
6 Can you remember any stories people have told you — true or made up?
7 Can you remember any newspaper stories?
8 Has anyone ever told you a story to scare you, or to warn you of anything? (Look back at the starters opposite.)

Make a list of stories you know. The list will help you to choose a story to write later on in this section.

Discussion and Notes

What makes a good story?
What were the best stories you heard? What made them better than the rest?
You have heard enough stories from books, films, TV, and stories people tell, to give good advice to storytellers and writers.

Write down all the things you think make a good story. Share your list with other members of the class, and add their ideas to yours if you agree with them.

Keep a copy of the class list in your exercise book or folder so that you can look at it during the year to try to improve your own stories, before you write your final versions.

Some stories give the reader a puzzle — and then the writer solves the puzzle with a clever, unexpected explanation. It's the surprise that makes the story worth telling.

Back to Front

"Reasonable people always see things in the same way," said the Khan of Samarkand to Nasrudin one day.

"That is just the trouble with 'reasonable people'," said Nasrudin. "They can only see one possibility where two may exist."

The Khan called all his wise men together to explain what this meant, but they thought Nasrudin was talking nonsense.

The next day Nasrudin rode through the town on a donkey in such a way that his face was towards its tail.

When he arrived at the palace where the Khan was sitting with his advisers, Nasrudin said:

"Would your Highness please ask these people what they have just seen?"

When asked, they all said: "A man riding back to front on a donkey."

"That is exactly my point," said Nasrudin. "The trouble with them all is that they did not notice that perhaps it was me who was right and the donkey that was the wrong way round."

adapted from *Caravan of Dreams* by Idries Shah

Reasonable or back to front reasons?

Can you think of reasonable explanations for these situations — and then think of some back to front reasons for the same pictures:

Retelling Stories

The story of Abu Nuwasi and the two thieves is very detailed. But because all the details fit together and each part of the story follows on from the next, it's quite easy to remember.

First, listen to the story. Then try to retell it.

Abu Nuwasi and the Two Thieves

One day Abu Nuwasi bought a sheep at the market and took it home with him. Then a thief jumped out of the bushes and started beating the old gentleman with a stick. While Abu Nuwasi defended himself, another thief appeared and ran away with the sheep. Then the first thief vanished too. When he had recovered from the beating, Abu Nuwasi got up, dusted himself, said Allabu Alimu (God is knowing) and went home.

There he thought up a plan to get his own back. Near the place where the two thieves operated there was a forest, and in the forest there was a large tree. Abu Nuwasi went up to the tree, climbed on to one of its lowest branches and reached for one of the gourds. He cut a hole in it, pushed some gold coins in the hole and closed it, taking care that the fruit remained fixed to the tree. He did the same with several other gourds and then climbed down. He had his bed placed right under the tree, lay down on it, and ordered armed guards to watch beside him.

Soon the two thieves arrived on the scene and asked him why he was sleeping under the tree. He replied that he was guarding his gold tree.

"Your what?"

"My tree with the gold-bearing fruit that my father has left me in his will."

"Sell it to us."

"I cannot sell it. It is my family property."

The thieves went away, rounded up a hundred head of cattle, then came back and said, "We want to buy this tree for a hundred cows, but you must first prove to us that the fruits contain gold."

Abu Nuwasi agreed, and instructed one of his guards to climb up and cut down some of the fruit from the lowest branch.

The thieves cut open the gourds and found lovely golden dinars in them. So they bought the tree, and together with the guards, Abu Nuwasi drove the cattle to his house.

When it was harvesting time, the two thieves climbed the tree with big knives and cut down all the fruit. They were enraged not to find a single coin in them, and they decided to go to Abu Nuwasi and claim their cattle.

Now Abu Nuwasi was a man of great knowledge, which had enabled him to read in the stars that they were coming to take their revenge, so he laid his plans carefully.

He went into the bush and caught two gazelles which looked exactly the same, were the same size, shape, colour, everything. Next he slaughtered an ox, cut out its bladder and filled it with blood. Then he told his wife:

"Put on a metal breast-plate, such as warriors wear, hang the bladder full of blood in front, and put on your usual dress over that. When the two thieves arrive, tell them I am in the fields, and when they have gone to find me there, cook the ox and prepare a good meal."

He locked up one of the gazelles, and took the other one with him.

Soon the two thieves found him in the fields, and claimed their cattle back because they said Abu Nuwasi had cheated them.

He said, "All right, all right, but first let us go to my house and have a good meal." Then he addressed the gazelle, saying: "You, my messenger, go and tell my wife to cook a good meal for my guests." He released the gazelle, which ran away into the bush and was never seen again.

The two thieves walked up to Abu Nuwasi's house and when they arrived there the meal was ready. Abu Nuwasi spoke sharply to his wife, saying the meal was not good enough for such distinguished guests. The wife talked back, they started shouting, and Abu Nuwasi worked up a temper saying: "I will teach you manners, you cheeky woman!" He drew his dagger and thrust it into her breast. Blood poured out and the wife fell flat on the floor. Then Abu Nuwasi went to the cupboard, took out a stick and touched his wife's breast with it, mumbling words in a strange tongue. Then he said: "Now rise again, woman, rise from the dead and I will forgive you." The wife rose up and the two thieves were deeply impressed.

They said, "We want to buy that clever gazelle-messenger of yours, and also your stick that wakes up the dead. We will give you a thousand dinars for it." Abu Nuwasi agreed and the thieves went away with the magic stick (or so they thought) and also with the other gazelle which Abu Nuwasi produced from where it had been locked up. The thieves did not realise that it was not the same animal.

On their way the two thieves started arguing about the problem of how to share out their new belongings. They quarrelled ever more heatedly until one of the two took out his big knife and stabbed the other one in the breast. Blood poured from the wound and he fell dead on the spot. The murderer felt sorry that he had killed his friend, took the stick and touched the dead body with it, but nothing happened — for a corpse is a corpse. He soon realised that he had forgotten to buy the magic words as well, so he went back to Abu Nuwasi to ask him to teach him the special words.

Abu Nuwasi had foreseen that one thief would come back so he had called the local police and asked them to hide. When the thief arrived, he told him what had happened and claimed the right to the formula which, he said, was part of the magic that belonged to the reviving stick. As soon as he had finished his story the police officers emerged and arrested him. They had heard everything. They found the corpse and the thief was hanged for murder.

Never harm a clever one.

from Myths and Legends of the Swahili by Jan Knappert

Ways of Retelling Stories

Retell the story in as much detail as you can. Choose **one** of these ways of retelling it.

☆ One person in the group has the job of "stopping and starting". He or she begins by calling the name of someone in the group. This person has to start telling the story of Abu Nuwasi, until the leader calls another name. When your name is called, you have to carry on from exactly where the last storyteller left off. (Don't give each other too long.)

Try to see which group in the class can make the story last the longest.

☆ Play the "stopping and starting game", but tell the story as if you were one of the thieves.

☆ Act out the story.
You need four main characters and some police. Think how you will present the characters. Is Abu Nuwasi a good man or a cheat? Does his wife help to work out the plot, or does she just do as she is told? Are the thieves stupid, or is Abu Nuwasi very clever?

☆ Another way of retelling the story is to answer these questions:
1 What did the thieves steal from Abu Nuwasi?
2 What did Abu Nuwasi do to make the thieves think the tree was a gold tree?
3 What did the thieves pay for the gold tree?
4 What did Abu Nuwasi do with the two gazelles?
5 What did Abu Nuwasi and his wife pretend to quarrel about?
6 What happened when Abu Nuwasi attacked his wife with a dagger?
7 What two things did Abu Nuwasi do to "raise his wife from the dead"?
8 How did the first thief die?
9 Why did the other thief go back to Abu Nuwasi?
10 How did the second thief die?

The Legend of Alderley

The way a story begins can often help us to guess what sort of story it is going to be. Listen to the opening of this story.

At dawn one still October day in the long ago of the world, across the hill of Alderley, a farmer from Mobberley was riding to Macclesfield fair.

The morning was dull, but mild; light mists bedimmed his way; the woods were hushed; the day promised fine. The farmer was in good spirits, and he let his horse, a milk-white mare, set her own pace, for he wanted her to arrive fresh for the market. A rich man would go back to Mobberley that night.

So, his mind in the town when he was yet on the hill, the farmer drew near to the place known as Thieves' Hole. And there the horse stood still and would answer to neither spur nor rein. The spur and rein she understood, and her master's stern

command, but the eyes that held her were stronger than all of these.

Make some guesses about what is going to happen. Find words or phrases that back up your guesses. Listen to the opening again: **what kind of story is this likely to be?**

Now listen to the rest of the story, and try retelling it in one of the ways suggested above.

9

In the middle of the path, where surely there had been no-one, was an old man, tall, with long hair and beard. "You go to sell this mare," he said. "I come here to buy. What is your price?"

But the farmer wished to sell only at the market, where he would have the choice of many offers, so he rudely bade the stranger quit the path and let him through, for if he stayed longer he would be late for the fair.

"Then go your way," said the old man. "None will buy. And I shall await you here at sunset."

The next moment he was gone, and the farmer could not tell how or where.

The day was warm, and the tavern cool, and all who saw the mare agreed that she was a splendid animal, the pride of Cheshire, a queen among horses; and everyone said that there was no finer beast in the town that day. But no-one offered to buy. A weary, sour-eyed farmer rode up out of Macclesfield as the sky reddened in the west.

At Thieves' Hole the mare would not budge: the stranger was there.

Thinking any price now better than none, the farmer agreed to sell. "How much will you give?" he said.

"Enough. Now come with me."

By Seven Firs and Golderstone they went, to Stormy Point and Saddlebole. And they halted before a great rock embedded in the hillside. The old man lifted his staff and lightly touched the rock and it split with the noise of thunder.

At this the farmer toppled from his plunging horse, and, on his knees, begged the other to have mercy on him and let him go on his way unharmed. The horse should stay; he did not want her. Only spare his life, that was enough.

The wizard, for such he was, commanded the farmer to rise. "I promise you safe conduct," he said. "Do not be afraid; for living wonders you shall see here."

Beyond the rock stood a pair of iron gates. These the wizard opened, and took the farmer and his horse down a narrow tunnel deep into the hill. A light, subdued but beautiful, marked the way. The passage ended, and they stepped into a cave, and there a wondrous sight met the farmer's eyes, a hundred and forty knights in silver armour and by the side of all but one a milk-white mare.

"Here they lie in an enchanted sleep," said the wizard, "until a day will come — and it will come — when England shall be in direst peril, and England's mothers weep. Then out from the hill these must ride and, in a battle thrice lost, thrice won, upon the plain, drive the enemy into the sea.

The farmer, dumb with awe, turned with the wizard into a further cavern, and here mounds of gold and silver and precious stones lay strewn along the ground.

"Take what you can carry in payment for the horse."

And when the farmer had crammed his pockets (ample as his lands), his shirt, and his fists with jewels, the wizard hurried him up the long tunnel and thrust him out of the gates. The farmer stumbled, the thunder rolled, he looked and there was only the bare rock face above him. He was alone on the hill, near Stormy Point. The broad full moon was up, and it was night.

And although in later years he tried to find the place, neither he nor any after him ever saw the iron gates again.

from *The Weirdstone of Brisingamen* by Alan Garner

Your Writing

Now you are going to choose one or two stories to write. They need not be long stories, but they should be well told, and enjoyable for other people to read.

The Stages of Writing

Choosing

These questions will help you to choose a story to write:

1 Which story did you retell best: Abu Nuwasi? The Legend?
2 Look at your list of "**Stories you know**" (page 5). Will you write one or two of these, or will you make up a new story?
3 Which story will the rest of the class enjoy most?

Planning

Make a list of the main events of your story.
Put them in the order you want to tell them.
Read your class's advice about **What makes a good story** (page 5).
Remember this advice when you are writing.

Drafting

Now write your story.
You can make changes at this stage — cross out neatly or write in pencil and rub out to improve your story as you go along.

Revising

Read your story and give it to someone else to read. These questions will help you to make improvements:

1 Is it easy to understand?
2 Do you want to add any details to catch the reader's interest?
3 Do you want to change the order of events?
4 Do you want to leave out any passages?
5 Do you want to put in more paragraphs?
6 Do you want to change any sentences that sound awkward, so that they read more naturally?
7 Can you think of better words to express your ideas more dramatically?

Proofreading

Proofreading means searching for any mistakes you made because you were working quickly and thinking of what to write next.
Search for:

1 Words missed out
2 Spelling mistakes
3 Full stops missed out
4 Capital letters missed out
5 Speech marks missed out
6 Sentences that aren't complete
7 Any other slips you can find

Presentation

Write out your story with all the changes you have made, clearly and correctly for other people to read.

Other things to do

Presenting your work

Draw pictures and a title page for your story.

Writing

Write a modern version of the story of Abu Nuwasi. The cartoon may help you.

Reading

Make a class anthology of stories, or a large wall display so that other people can spend time reading what you have written.

The Stages of Writing

When you wrote stories in the last section of the book, you wrote them in five stages:

Stage 1 Planning

Getting ideas.
Putting them in order.

Stage 2 Drafting

Writing your first version.
Concentrating on what to write.

Stage 3 Revising

Reading your work and trying it out on friends to make it better.

Stage 4 Proofreading

Finding your mistakes and correcting them.

Stage 5 Presentation

Writing out the final version. Making it look clear and attractive for other people to read.

Follow these stages when you want your writing to be at its best. You will get quicker at drafting and revising with practice.

Before you start writing you need to gather your ideas. Ideas come from all your experiences.

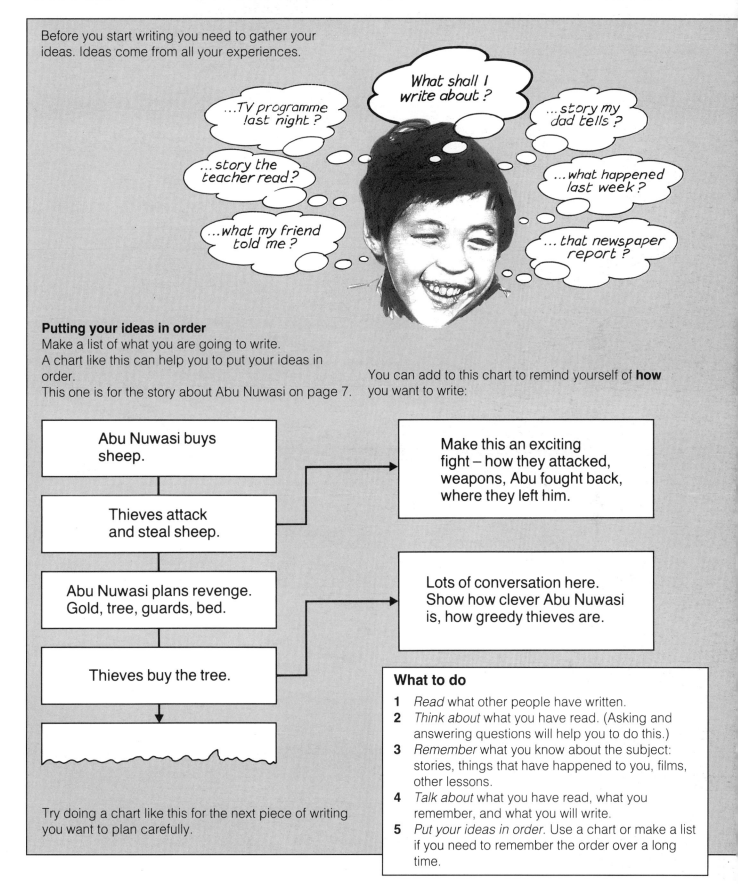

What shall I write about?

...TV programme last night?

...story my dad tells?

...story the teacher read?

...what happened last week?

...what my friend told me?

...that newspaper report?

Putting your ideas in order

Make a list of what you are going to write.
A chart like this can help you to put your ideas in order.
This one is for the story about Abu Nuwasi on page 7.

You can add to this chart to remind yourself of **how** you want to write:

Abu Nuwasi buys sheep.

Thieves attack and steal sheep.

→ Make this an exciting fight – how they attacked, weapons, Abu fought back, where they left him.

Abu Nuwasi plans revenge. Gold, tree, guards, bed.

Thieves buy the tree.

→ Lots of conversation here. Show how clever Abu Nuwasi is, how greedy thieves are.

Try doing a chart like this for the next piece of writing you want to plan carefully.

What to do

1 *Read* what other people have written.
2 *Think about* what you have read. (Asking and answering questions will help you to do this.)
3 *Remember* what you know about the subject: stories, things that have happened to you, films, other lessons.
4 *Talk about* what you have read, what you remember, and what you will write.
5 *Put your ideas in order.* Use a chart or make a list if you need to remember the order over a long time.

Drafting

Now write the first version of your
piece of writing. It might
look like this:

~~The school was modern but a bit of it was old.~~
~~There was one block that was older.~~ it was
~~The old block was gloomy and the lighting~~
~~wasn't very good.~~

The school was a modern one, but one of
the blocks was older than the others. It was a
tall, gloomy
~~gloomy~~ building and ~~the lighting wasn't very~~
~~good~~ and at night the cold fluorescent
lights/cast an eerie glow over the corridors.

My classroom was on the ~~highest~~ top floor, and after
the cleaners ~~had left~~ had left in the evenings,
it was always ~~empty~~ deserted. I never
~~wanted.~~ Nobody ever wanted to do detention
there. But it wasn't just the ~~loneliness and~~ cold
and the loneliness that made us hurry out
of 'E' block . . . . .
The English teachers always told the first years
a ~~legend~~ ghost story; but . . . . well . . . .
The teachers said that years before the old
block had been a girls' boarding school.
top floor ~~had held~~ had been arranged

What to do

1 Writing your first version means *making changes* as you go along.
2 *Keep a separate notebook*, or a separate part of your exercise book for your first drafts.
3 *Write on alternate lines* to leave space for improvements.
4 *Write in pencil* or a pen you can rub out.
5 Don't be afraid to *score out neatly and start again*.

Stage 3   Revising

Revising means reading what you have written very carefully, and finding ways to improve it. If you revise your work with a partner, you can help each other.

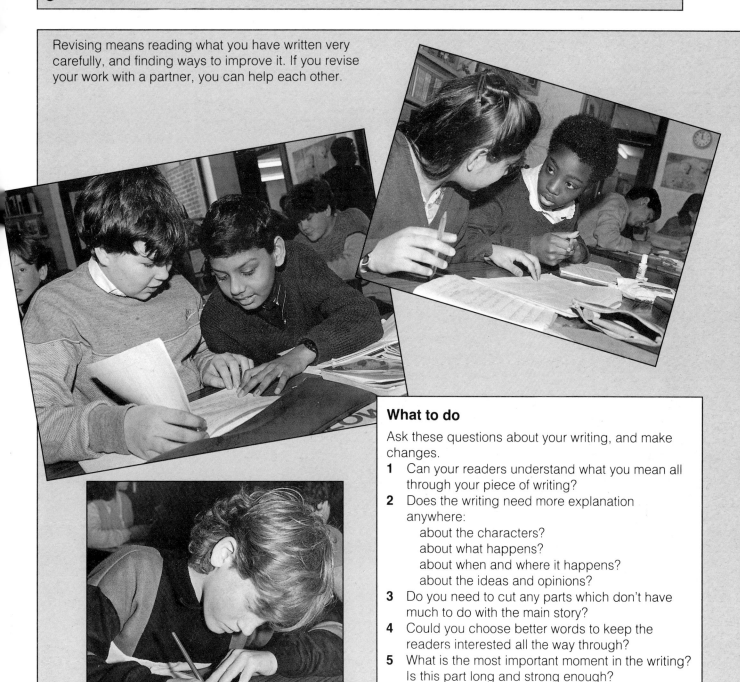

What to do

Ask these questions about your writing, and make changes.

1   Can your readers understand what you mean all through your piece of writing?
2   Does the writing need more explanation anywhere:
    about the characters?
    about what happens?
    about when and where it happens?
    about the ideas and opinions?
3   Do you need to cut any parts which don't have much to do with the main story?
4   Could you choose better words to keep the readers interested all the way through?
5   What is the most important moment in the writing? Is this part long and strong enough? Does it need more detail?
6   Think about the title and purpose of this particular piece of writing. What is the purpose? Has the writing succeeded in this purpose? For example:
    Is it meant to be a sad story?
    Is it sad enough?
    Is it meant to be a clear description?
    Is it clear enough?
    Have you described the important things?
7   Could you help the reader to understand what you have written by putting in more paragraphs?
(Turn to page 19 for help.)

Stage 4 Proofreading

Proofreading means searching for any mistakes you have made because you were writing quickly.

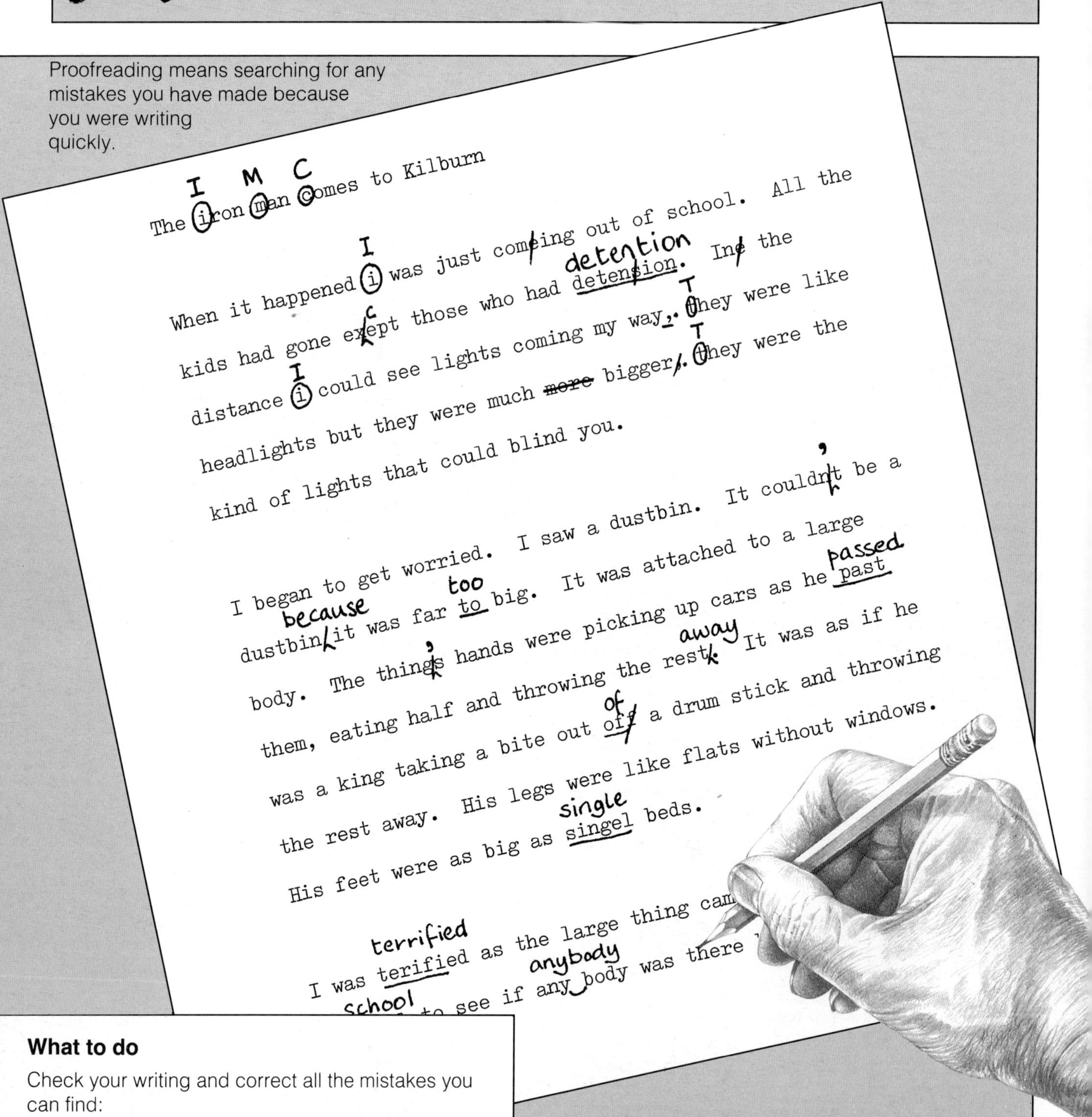

The ⓘron ⓜan ⓒomes to Kilburn
(I M C above)

When it happened ⓘ was just coming out of school. All the

kids had gone exept those who had ~~detension~~ detention. In~~e~~ the
(C below exept; I above happened; detention written above detension)

distance ⓘ could see lights coming my way~~.~~, ~~t~~hey were like
(T above)

headlights but they were much ~~more~~ bigger~~.~~. ~~t~~hey were the
(T above)

kind of lights that could blind you.

I began to get worried. I saw a dustbin. It couldn't be a
(apostrophe added couldn't)

                              too
dustbin ^because ~~it~~ was far ~~to~~ big. It was attached to a large
                                                            passed
body. The thing's hands were picking up cars as he ~~past~~
                                         away
them, eating half and throwing the rest^. It was as if he
                                of
was a king taking a bite out ~~off~~ a drum stick and throwing

the rest away. His legs were like flats without windows.
                                 single
His feet were as big as ~~singel~~ beds.

       terrified
I was ~~terified~~ as the large thing cam...
school   anybody
       ...to see if any body was there ...

What to do

Check your writing and correct all the mistakes you can find:

1 Sentences that aren't complete
2 Full stops missing (turn to page 19 for help)
3 Capital letters missing
4 Speech marks missing (turn to page 20 for help)
5 Words missed out
6 Slips of the pen — spelling mistakes you can easily correct yourself
7 Spelling words you are not sure of (use a dictionary if you have some idea; otherwise, ask)

Stage 5 Presentation

When you are satisfied with your writing, you may want other people to read and enjoy it.

You need to present it attractively so that people's attention is drawn to it, and so that they can read and understand it clearly.

Your title Think about your title. Make it interesting and striking. (Look at newspaper headlines for ideas.)

Write it large and clear in big letters. Here are some ideas.

IRON MAN SHOCK

Sub-headings If the writing is long, does it need splitting into different parts?

If so, give each part its own title, or, sub-heading. Usually sub-headings go at the side of the page.

Spacing Space your work out generously.

Allow plenty of space for titles and sub-headings. Leave a line between paragraphs.

If the writing is short, set it out in the middle of the page and draw wide margins round it.

Handwriting Keep your handwriting large and clear.

Think as you write. Make any changes that will improve your writing.

Correct any mistakes you noticed —- and look out in case there are more.

Iron Man Comes to Kilburn

THE KILBURN IRON MAN

KILBURN HORROR!

The Iron Man comes to Kilburn

When it happened I was just coming out of school. All the kids had gone except those who had detention. In the distance I could see lights coming my way. They were like headlights but they were much bigger. They were the kind that could blind you.

I began to get worried. I saw a dustbin. It couldn't be a dustbin because it was far too big. It was attached to a large body. The thing's hands were picking up cars as he passed them. It was as if he was eating half and throwing the rest away. It was as if he was taking a bite out of a drum stick and throwing the rest away. His feet were as if they were flats without windows. His legs were as if they were as big as single beds.

I was terrified as the large thing came my way. I ran back to school to see if anybody was there but everyone had gone. I started to . . . . .

Illustrations If you have time, illustrate your writing in one of these ways:

Do your own drawings.

Collect suitable pictures from newspapers, magazines, comics, cards or make photocopies of illustrations in books.

Decorate the margins and titles.

Make a "book jacket" for the writing with the title, your name, an illustration and a few tempting words for the reader.

Getting it Right

Contents

**Paragraphing   Sentences   Capital Letters   Conversation in a Story
                                                        Conversation in a Play**

Paragraphing

One of the ways in which a writer helps to make the meaning of the writing clear to the reader is by setting it out in paragraphs.

Compare the way this passage has been laid out, first without, and then with paragraphs. How do the paragraphs help to make the meaning clearer?

The Summer

The children had a very fine time during the summer holiday. They went to stay with their grandparents who lived near the sea. The weather was hot and sunny and they made friends with some children of their age who lived nearby. The coast there was rocky. At first they were disappointed because there was so little sand. Then they discovered that when the tide went out the rock pools were full of weird plants and strange creatures to capture in nets. One day their granny cooked the little shrimps they carried back in a bucket. They watched them turn pink. In the end they gave them to the cat because they couldn't face eating them. At the end of the holiday they had to go back to school. They discovered that they had a new teacher. "Did you have a good holiday?" she asked. "Yes, it was great," they replied, "better than being at school."

The Summer

The children had a very fine time during the summer holiday. They went to stay with their grandparents who lived near the sea. The weather was hot and sunny and they made friends with some children of their age who lived nearby.

The coast there was rocky. At first they were disappointed because there was so little sand. Then they discovered that when the tide went out the rock pools were full of weird plants and strange creatures to capture in nets.

One day their granny cooked the little shrimps they carried back in a bucket. They watched them turn pink. In the end they gave them to the cat because they couldn't face eating them.

At the end of the holiday they had to go back to school. They discovered that they had a new teacher.

"Did you have a good holiday?" she asked.

"Yes, it was great," they replied, "better than being at school."

1 How is the start of a new paragraph shown?
2 Why is the writing divided into paragraphs?
3 Make up a title for each of the first four paragraphs.

18

How to use paragraphs

1 You show the start of a new paragraph by starting a new line about one inch in from the margin. (There are different ways of showing a new paragraph. Often modern business letters leave a gap of a few lines, but start close to the margin.) Get in the habit of noticing how different printers set out paragraphs.

2 You start a new paragraph when you start to write about something new: perhaps a new part of the story

    when the time changes
    when the place changes
    when the person changes
    when the event changes
or a new part of the subject you are describing.

3 You start a new paragraph when someone new starts to talk.

4 These signs indicate that you should start a new paragraph. **NP** **⌐**
Choose one and use it when you are proof-reading your own or someone else's writing.

Just make all these points clear by proof-reading this short piece of writing and then presenting it properly written out in paragraphs.

How I Spend My Time

I have three pets at home, a hamster, a dog and a goldfish. Best of all I like the dog because he is more fun to play with, and I like taking him on walks. The hamster is all right, but I don't like the goldfish much, particularly as he has ugly spots on him and my mum says he is going to die soon. My chief hobby is cycling. I had a hard job to persuade dad to let me have a bike because he says it is dangerous in traffic. My longest ride in a day was 69 miles. School is not bad but teachers moan too much. "Why are you late?" says my teacher to me nearly every day. "Because I got up late," I reply.

Sentences and full stops

As you read over your writing, check carefully that you haven't missed any full stops. Full stops divide the writing into sentences.

Read this piece of writing which has no full stops and decide where they should be. Where, as you read, do you need to stop because something new is starting?

Press Gang

a press gang waits in the shadows a man walks down the street one of the gang steps out in front of him the man tries to pass but the sailor whistles the gang suddenly appears the man tries to run for it but he is caught and overpowered the gang hold his arms and carry him off helpless, twisting and shouting

Rules for sentences

1 A piece of writing is divided into sentences to make the meaning clear.
2 A sentence ends when one complete thing has been said and a new idea is starting.

Try one more to get the idea:

The Sheep Rustlers

when all the sheep were in the lorry the rustlers drove off the girl did not say anything she went downstairs and woke up her dad her dad was really mad to be woken up and thought she was playing about he told her that they'd sort it out in the morning she told her brothers and sisters all about it and then went to sleep in the morning all the children went out and the field was empty dad came out and complained that she hadn't told him properly

Capital Letters

Try putting all the capital letters and full stops in this passage:

the book i enjoyed most

the book i enjoyed most was "stig of the dump" my friend jane liked the bit where the snargets, william tell, robin hood and the lone ranger captured barney that was all right but i liked the bit when they went to mrs fawkham-greene's and lou was nearly eaten by a leopard after that miss holland read us "tower by the sea"

Now write the rules for using capital letters. Check them against the summary below.

Proofread this passage to check the rules.

a visit to the science museum

on tuesday my mother, mrs elliot, took my brother and me to the science museum my brother paul is a bookworm he bought the book "jaws" on finsbury park station we took the train to south kensington when we got there we found that the museum was closed on tuesdays and sundays, so mother took us to trafalgar square instead

the canal ghost

this story begins one hundred years ago on the grand union canal the canal boats had no motors so when they came to a tunnel the men had to push the boats through with their feet one day a man was crushed to death his foot had got caught and that was how he was crushed now men were frightened to steer the boat into tunnels like this and many others so the women had to steer the boats through the tunnels now there was a man and his wife called fred and sue fred's wife sue steered the boat through the tunnels until she died after her death he was steering the boat he saw a tunnel ahead all of a sudden he heard a voice say "go downstairs I will steer the boat" "is that you sue" "yes now go down" now when fred comes to a tunnel the ghost of his wife sue steers the boat for him.

When to use Capital Letters
1 The beginning of each new sentence
2 Names of people
3 Names of places and dates
4 Titles of books, stories and films
5 "I" meaning "myself".

Conversation in a Story

There are three rules to remember. Here's a famous writer, Sid Chaplin, who's broken one of them. He's telling a story about an old man who has just had a serious accident running for a bus. The only person who wants to help is Dick who goes for a doctor. The bus driver gets fed up with waiting for Dick to come back, so puts the old man in the bus and drives to the doctor's. The conversation takes place between the bus driver and Dick in the street outside the doctor's surgery.

Dick ran over to the bus. The driver met him. "Been a time, haven't you?" the driver said. "Doctor didn't want to come," said Dick. "Where is the old man?" "In the bus," said the driver. "Got fed-up of waiting so we dumped him inside." "What's he like?" asked Dick. The driver got out of the cab. "Going, going, nearly gone," he said. "Come on!" "What are we going to do?" said Dick. "Carry him over to the surgery," said the driver. "But what about the doctor. . . ." said Dick. "To hell with him," said the driver. "I'm late as it is. Haven't time to argue with the blooming doctor."

1 What rule does Sid Chaplin break?
2 Look at the writing. Do you know what the other two rules are?

How to set out conversation in a story
1 When somebody new starts to speak, start a new paragraph.
2 Put speech marks before and after the words that are said.
3 Put punctuation, (a comma, full stop, question mark, or exclamation mark) after the words that are said.

Write out the passage correctly. Start like this:

Dick ran over to the bus. The driver met him.
"Been a hell of a time, haven't you?" the driver said.
"Doctor didn't want to come," said Dick. "Where is the old man?"
"In the bus," said the driver. "Got fed-up of waiting so we dumped him inside."
"What's he like?" asked Dick.

Conversation in a Play

If Sid Chaplin had written his story as a play he might have written it out like this. Look at it carefully and see if you can work out the rules for setting out a play.

The Unwanted

Characters: Bus driver
Dick

Scene: The street outside a doctor's house
(Dick runs over to speak to the bus driver.)

Bus driver: (angrily) Been a time, haven't you?

Dick: Doctor didn't want to come. Where is the old man?

Bus driver: In the bus. Got fed up of waiting, so we dumped him inside.

Dick: What's he like?

Bus driver: (Getting out of his cab) Going, going, nearly gone! Come on!

How to set out conversation in a play
1 Give your play a title.
2 Write a list of your characters.
3 Describe the scene. Say where the play is taking place.
4 Explain the action, or how the characters speak, in "stage directions". Put these inside a pair of brackets. (*Printers also print them in italic, like this.*)
5 Put the speaker's name in the margin.
6 Put a colon (:) after the speaker's name.
7 **Don't** use speech marks.
8 Make sure there is proper punctuation at the end of each speech. It might be a full stop, question mark, or exclamation mark.

Put the rest of Sid Chaplin's story in a play.

Creation

Contents

Creating a World
    The Big Rock Candy Mountain
    The Creation of My World
    Your Writing: Description

Rules for a World
    In the Beginning
    The Boomerang
    Discussion and Writing
    The Devil in Texas
    Your Writing: Poems

The First Humans
    The Garden of Eden
    The Revolt against God

Other things to do
    A Perfect World
    Inventions
    Breaking Rules
    Making Things

Creating a World

The writers of the two pieces on these pages are creating new worlds in their imagination.

In the poem, an American hobo (a tramp) is making up the world he would like.

The Big Rock Candy Mountain

One evening as the sun went down
And the jungle fire was burning
Down the track came a hobo hiking,
And he said: "Boys, I'm not turning,
I'm headed for a land that's far away
Beside the crystal fountains,
So come with me, we'll all go see
The Big Rock Candy Mountains."

In the Big Rock Candy Mountains,
There's a land that's fair and bright,
Where the handouts grow on bushes,
And you sleep out every night.
Where the boxcars* are all empty,
And the sun shines every day
On the birds and the bees and the cigarette trees,
And the lemonade springs where the bluebird
   sings,
In the Big Rock Candy Mountains.

In the Big Rock Candy Mountains,
All the cops have wooden legs,
The bulldogs all have rubber teeth,
And the hens lay soft-boiled eggs.
The farmers' trees are full of fruit,
And the barns are full of hay.
Oh, I'm bound to go where there ain't no snow,
Where the rain don't pour, the wind don't blow,
In the Big Rock Candy Mountains.

In the Big Rock Candy Mountains,
You never change your socks,
And the little streams of alcohol
Come trickling down the rocks.
Then the brakemen have to tip their hats
And the railroad bulls are blind.
There's a lake of stew and of whisky too,
You can paddle all around 'em in a big canoe,
In the Big Rock Candy Mountains.

In the Big Rock Candy Mountains,
All the jails are made of tin,
And you can burst right out again
As soon as you are in.
There ain't no short-handled shovels,
No axes, saws or picks.
I'm going to stay where you sleep all day,
Where they hung the jerk who invented work,
In the Big Rock Candy Mountains.

boxcars–goods wagons

In this piece, Elaine describes making a world from the very beginning.

The Creation of My World

My world was burning hot. It had no shape, just one mass of flames. Steam was flying out of the world. It needed something to cool it down, so I made lakes and rivers. The world needed a shape so I made it circular. I got bored with plain ground all around me, so I made trees with blue leaves and white patches. The fruit and flowers on the trees were strange. They were green flowers with yellow stripes. And the fruit that grew on the trees were square and pink-coloured.

Then I decided what kind of people to put on the land. First I thought of people with animal's bodies and people's heads. But then I decided to have people that looked a bit like you or me, but instead of our heads they had the head of any animal that I thought would suit their personality.

If it was a stubborn person I made, it would have the head of a donkey. If their personality changed I would change their head. If someone changed into a good person they would be rewarded by being given a human's head.

They would be given a choice of homes, and would be left to argue among themselves who would have which house. Sometimes ten people would have to share one house. If they were bad they would be punished. If they were very bad or told lots of lies they would be struck by lightning. Sometimes when there was a flood, there wouldn't be enough shelter, so people would be carried away in the flood. Some would even drown.

Elaine Jackson (aged 11)

Your Writing: Description

In "*The Big Rock Candy Mountain*", the hobo tells us about an imaginary world that he would like to live in. Elaine Jackson describes how she created her imaginary world.

Start thinking about a piece of writing in which you "create a world".

Planning

1   The hobo wanted to make his life easier.
    Pick out all the things in a far away land which he was looking forward to.
    Make a chart like the one opposite and set out these ideas on the left of the chart.

2   Read Elaine's "*The Creation of My World*" again. She writes about some of the same things that the hobo wanted, and some new ideas. What are her new ideas? Add them to your chart.

3   Decide. Are you going to write:
       like the hobo, and describe a perfect world for you to live in?
       like Elaine, as if you are a god, creating a new world?
    Is your world going to be a fantasy, like Elaine's and the hobo's, or will it be more like real life?

4   Look through the list of ideas from the two pieces of writing. Which do you want to use? Which do you want to leave out? Which do you want to change? Jot down your ideas on the right hand side of the chart.

5   Add new thoughts of your own to your chart of ideas.

THINGS THE HOBO WANTED	MY IDEAS: IN MY WORLD
money growing on trees	money will be banned
sleep out every night	X can't use this
box cars empty	X can't use this
weather always fine	snow all the year
cigarette trees	bad for your health – leave out
lemonade springs	prefer coke
ELAINE'S IDEAS	
hot at the beginning	darkness at the beginning
shape	a cube?
plants	must provide enough food
NEW IDEAS	
school	there will be school – but better
transport	personal ground/air vehicles

Drafting

Use your chart of ideas to help you try out a piece of writing, "*Creating a World*".

Rules for a World

The next two stories are from Frazer Island, a large island off the coast of Queensland, Australia, the home of one group of aboriginals, the Butchulla.

Stories were told around the fire in the evenings. The stories explained the world, and gave lessons in rules for living. Those who knew the stories well didn't write them down, but drew them out to make a coloured decorative pattern, like a kind of comic strip. The pictures were not laid out in the order of the story, but in the order which gave the most pleasing pattern.

In the Beginning....

Beerall was the god of the Butchulla people. His name could never be spoken, and his sign was the rainbow. His son was Yindingie, and he appeared as the carpet snake.

Way back in the First Time, when the world was just made, Yindingie had to teach all the birds, animals and men how to live.

Then, as the years passed, the parents and old people taught the young ones the things Yindingie had said, such as:

You must never pass between a man and his fire. This means the man's dwelling and that of his family are his own private property.

It is also rude to sit down at a man's fire until you have been invited to do so.

To teach the children to stay in safe places, the parents told them the story of the jabirou and the leatherhead. The leatherhead stole the jabirou's fish, and the jabirou chased him. The leatherhead did not escape further down and it did not escape further up, and the jabirou hit the leatherhead with a burning stick.

When the children asked why the leatherhead had not escaped further down, they were told of the bog that was dangerous. When they asked why he had not escaped further up, they were told that it was dangerous too, because a Melong lived there.

While Yindingie was busy teaching the birds how to build nests, one little chap kept getting in the way and wanting to be shown how to build a nest.

Yindingie said to him, "You are a bat, not a bird."

"But," said the flying fox, "I have wings and I can fly. Why can't I build a nest too?"

Then he kept on making a nuisance of himself too till the Yindingie, becoming angry, picked him

This diagram shows the order of events in the picture opposite

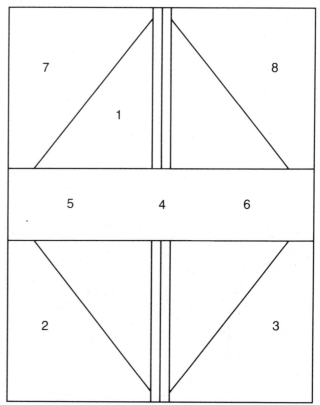

up, tied his feet together, and hung him head down over a limb. This made the others laugh.

Now, when they had finished for the day, the Yindingie came to him and said, "Now, have you had enough? Perhaps that will teach you a lesson."

"Oh, no!" said the flying fox. "I like it here. I like looking at the world like this. I think it is nice."

Then said Yindingie, "You shall always hang around like that."

Then he bent the flying fox's toes around so that he could hang by them to the limbs.

Of course the flying fox was only pretending. He really just didn't want the other birds to know how much he had been humiliated. You never see him now until all the other birds have gone to sleep, and when he goes to sleep in the daytime, he usually picks a hollow tree or a dark cave where no other birds can see him and laugh at him.

The Boomerang

A long time ago a little boy and girl were playing on the seashore. The boy was not yet old enough to begin the training that would lead eventually to his being received by the elders of the tribe as a warrior. Like most children of his age, he liked to show off.

Then he made a bad mistake. He killed a little bird that he should never have touched. In fact he should have made a special effort to protect it, for this was his "Eurie" — his "meat".

Each person has his own particular Eurie given him at birth, and it is regarded as his second self. Should you be hunting with someone whose Eurie is the duck you must first ask his permission before you kill any ducks, or run the risk of being impaled on the end of the duck man's spear!

It is Yindingie — the spirit god and messenger of the higher god Beerall — who, when you die, takes your spirit to the bottom of a certain lake. Here you pass a guard at the mouth of a cave, then on past two more guards to the end of the cave. After going through certain rites*, your spirit is ready for its journey into the east. Yindingie often comes to earth in the form of a large snake. You will remember that his sign is the rainbow.

Now when Yindingie saw what had happened he decided to punish the children. He came as a large serpent, picked up the children and began to swim out to sea. Hearing their cries the fighting men grabbed their spears and rushed to the beach. When they saw who it was they were afraid, that is all except one man, the father of the children. He threw his nulla-nulla. There was a great splash of water as it hit the serpent's head, glanced off, and came hurtling back towards him, and had he not stepped quickly aside, no doubt he would have been killed.

When next they looked towards where the splash had occurred, the Yindingie and the children were gone, and in their place stood two rocks side by side.

On picking up his nulla-nulla, the father found more disappointment. Not only had he lost his children, but here was his best nulla-nulla, the one he intended to use on the next full moon when there was to be a war with a neighbouring tribe. He had spent weeks "hardening" it and getting it just so, for he prided himself as a maker of fine weapons. Now here it was quite flattened and bent out of shape.

In disgust he threw it at the rocks. But even before it had reached halfway, it circled in the air and came back to rest at his feet.

*rites — ceremonies

Discussion and Writing

Thinking about Rules
Talk about or jot down answers to these four points:
1 What were the rules that Yindingie and the parents taught their children?
2 For each rule, say why you think it was important for the parents to tell the children this.
3 Think whether you have ever been given a similar rule.
4 What do you think are the important rules that you have been given? Make a list of them and put them in the order of their importance.

The Rules of Your World
Work out the list of rules you would want everybody to follow in a world you created. Think about an interesting way of presenting it. One way would be to do it as a picture story.

The Boomerang
Tell in your own words how the boomerang was invented.

In many stories about the creation, somebody or something comes along who spoils everything. Read this poem about how the Devil spoils Texas.

The Devil in Texas

He scattered tarantulas over the roads,
Put thorns on the cactus and horns on the toads,
He sprinkled the sands with millions of ants
So the man who sits down must wear soles on his
    pants.
He lengthened the horns of the Texas steer,
And added an inch to the jack rabbit's ear;
He put mouths full of teeth in all of the lakes,
And under the rocks he put rattlesnakes.

He hung thorns and brambles on all of the trees,
He mixed up the dust with jiggers and fleas;
The rattlesnake bites you, the scorpion stings,
The mosquito delights you by buzzing his wings.
The heat in the summer's a hundred and ten,
Too hot for the Devil and too hot for men;
And all who remain in that climate soon bear
Cuts, bites, and stings, from their feet to their
    hair.

He quickened the buck of the bronco steed,
And poisoned the feet of the centipede;
The wild boar roams in the black chaparral;
It's a hell of a place that we've got for a hell.
He planted red pepper beside every brook;
The Mexicans use them in all that they cook.
Just dine with a Mexican, then you will shout,
"I've hell on the inside as well as the out!"

Anon

Your Writing: Poems

Make your own list of the things that are wrong with a place you know well, for example
   your town; your school; your street.
Then write a poem blaming the Devil for all these things.
   Each item in your list becomes a line of your poem.
Decide whether you want to make the lines rhyme in pairs or not.

The First Humans

Here are two stories about the first humans in the world. As you read them, think about how the stories are similar.

The first is a version of the story told in the Bible.

The Garden of Eden

One day Lord Yahweh formed a man from mud and breathed life into him. Yahweh called him Adam — the Hebrew word for "man". Realising that Adam would have to have somewhere to live, Yahweh planted a garden in the East and called it Eden. He made all kinds of trees and plants spring up, so that the garden was sheltered to live in and beautiful to look at, and there was plenty of fruit for Adam to eat. Right in the middle of the garden, Yahweh planted two special trees — the Tree of Life and the Tree of Knowledge. Anyone who ate the fruit from the Tree of Life would live for ever, and anyone eating the fruit of the Tree of Knowledge would immediately be able to tell the difference between right and wrong.

When the garden was ready, Yahweh set Adam down gently in the garden to look after it.

"Here you are — this is your home," Yahweh told him. "There are lots of good things to eat, but keep away from that tree in the middle of the garden. That is the Tree of Knowledge, and if you eat any of its fruit, you will die."

At that time, although Adam was a fully grown man, he was as innocent as a baby, and went about naked.

After a while, Yahweh realised that Adam was lonely in the great garden all by himself. First of all, Yahweh shaped all the wild animals and birds out of the mud, brought them to life, and let Adam choose names for them all. But still Adam had no-one to talk to. Yahweh decided he would have to make a mate for Adam.

That night, while Adam was asleep, Yahweh made a woman, and when Adam woke up he was very pleased to see his companion.

One of the cleverest of the animals in the garden was the snake. One day, he was talking to the woman.

"I hear you're not allowed to eat any of the fruit from the trees in the garden," he hissed slyly.

"Oh yes, we can," the woman replied innocently. "We can eat any of the fruit we like, except the fruit of the tree in the middle of the garden. The

Lord Yahweh told us that if we eat that, we shall die."

"Of course you wouldn't die," the snake scoffed. "That's the Tree of Knowledge, silly. If you were to eat the fruit of that tree, you'd become a god, like Lord Yahweh himself. That's why he doesn't want you to eat it."

The woman looked at the fruit on the Tree of Knowledge and it really did look quite harmless. The more she thought about it, the more tempted she was. She went up to the tree, put out her hand — then pulled it back in fear.

"Go on — what harm can it do?" hissed the snake.

The woman reached out again, took an apple from the tree, and hesitantly took a bite. It seemed harmless enough, just as the snake had said. She took some to Adam, and he tasted it too. At first nothing was different. Then, gradually, the fruit began to take effect. The first thing they realised was that they were both naked; it hadn't mattered before, but now, suddenly, it seemed wrong, so they made themselves simple loincloths out of leaves.

Just then, as the evening breeze began to rustle through the trees, they heard Lord Yahweh walking through the garden towards them. The man and woman looked at each other guiltily. What had they done? Surely Yahweh would find out and punish them. Adam took the woman's hand and hid among the trees.

"Adam! Where are you?" called Yahweh.

Sheepishly, Adam came out from the trees and walked towards Yahweh.

"Adam — what's the matter?" asked Yahweh. "Why were you hiding?"

"I heard you coming, and I was frightened because I hadn't any clothes on, so I went and hid behind a tree," said Adam lamely.

"Clothes?" said Yahweh sternly. "Who told you about clothes? Have you been eating the fruit of the Tree of Knowledge — the fruit I expressly told you not to eat?"

"It was the woman's fault!" said Adam accusingly. "That woman you made to be my mate! She gave it to me."

Yahweh looked at the woman, who by this time had come out from her hiding place and was standing next to Adam with downcast eyes.

"What have you to say for yourself?" Yahweh asked her.

"It was the snake — he tricked me, and I ate the fruit," the woman answered.

Yahweh drew himself up and looked scornfully down at the unhappy pair. They shuffled their feet and waited for Yahweh's verdict. Yahweh saw through their flimsy excuses. First of all, he addressed the snake.

"You miserable creature! Because of this act of yours, you shall be different from all other animals from now on. You shall crawl and slither about on your stomach, and eat dirt for the rest of your life. Everyone will hate and mistrust you — particularly this woman and her children. They will strike out at your head whenever they see you, and you will strike at their heels."

Then Yahweh turned to the woman.

"Your punishment is even worse. When you have children, it will be agonisingly painful for you. And you will not be able to avoid having children."

Finally, Yahweh spoke to Adam.

"There is no excuse for your disobedience. You listened to the woman, and ate the forbidden fruit.

Because of you, I curse the land on which you are standing. No more will you live a life of leisure here in the garden. If you want to eat, you will have to dig and sow, and struggle to grow food for the rest of your days. Thistles and thorns will choke your crops, and you will have to work on the land until the day you die and are buried. You were made from dust, and to dust you will return."

Because the woman was to become the mother of the human race, Adam called her Eve — Hebrew for "life". Yahweh made clothes for Adam and Eve out of animal skins, while he pondered what to do with them.

"Man has become like one of the gods — he has the power of knowledge," he mused. "What if he were to eat the fruit of the Tree of Life as well? Then he would live for ever! I cannot let them stay here in the garden — it is too dangerous."

So Lord Yahweh drove Adam and Eve out of the Garden of Eden for ever, and barred the entrance to the garden with sharp swords so that mankind could never return.

from *Gods and Men* by John Bailey, slightly adapted

The second story about the first humans is from Gabon, on the west coast of Africa.

The Revolt against God

At the beginning of things, when there was nothing, neither man, nor animals, nor plants, nor heaven, nor earth, nor nothing, nothing, God **was** and he was called Nzame, Mebere, and Nkwa. At the beginning Nzame made the heaven and the earth and he reserved the heaven for himself. Then he blew onto the earth, and earth and water were created, each on its side.

Nzame made everything: heaven, earth, sun, moon, stars, animals, plants; everything. When he had finished everything that we see today, he called Mebere and Nkwa and showed them his work.

"This is my work. Is it good?"

They replied, "Yes, you have done well."

"Does anything remain to be done?"

Mebere and Nkwa answered him, "We see many animals, but we do not see their chief; we see many plants, but we do not see their master."

So Nzame, Mebere, and Nkwa created a being almost like themselves. One gave him strength, the second power, and the third beauty.

Then the three of them said:

"Take the earth. You are henceforth the master of all that exists. Like us you have life, all things belong to you, you are the master."

Nzame, Mebere and Nkwa returned to the heights to their dwelling-place, and the new creature remained below alone, and everything obeyed him. Nzame, Mebere, and Nkwa called the first man *Fam* — which means power.

Proud of his strength, his power and his beauty, and proud of being able to defeat all the animals, the first man grew wicked; he became arrogant, and did not want to worship Nzame again: and he scorned him:

Yeye, o layeye,
God on high, man on the earth,
Yeye, o layeye,
God is God,
Man is man,
Everyone in his house, everyone for himself!

God heard the song. "Who sings?" he asked.

"Look for him," cried Fam.

"Who sings?"

"Yeye, o, layeye!"

"Who sings?"

"Eh! It is me!" cried Fam.

Furious, God called Nzalan, the thunder. "Nzalan, come!"

Nzalan came running with great noise: *boom, boom, boom!* The fire of heaven fell on the forest. The plantations burnt like vast torches. *Foo, foo, foo!* — everything in flames. The earth was then as today, covered with forests. The trees burnt, the plants, the bananas, the cassava, even the pistachio nuts, everything dried up; animals, birds, fishes, all were destroyed, everything was dead. But when God had created the first man, he had told him, "You will never die." And what God gives, he does not take away. The first man was burnt, but none knows what became of him. He is alive, yes, but where?

But God looked at all the earth, all black, without anything, and idle; he felt ashamed, and wanted to do better. Nzame, Mebere, and Nkwa took counsel and they did as follows: over the black earth covered with coal they put a new layer of earth, a tree grew, grew bigger and bigger and when one of its seeds fell down a new tree was born, and when a leaf severed itself it grew and grew and began to walk. It was an animal, an elephant, a leopard, an antelope, a tortoise — all of them. When a leaf fell into the water it swam, it was a fish, a sardine, a crab, an oyster — all of them. The earth became again what it had been, and what it still is today. The proof that this is the truth is this: when one digs up the earth in certain places, one finds a hard black stone which breaks; throw it into the fire and it burns.

But Nzame, Mebere, and Nkwa took counsel again; they needed a chief to command all the animals. "We shall make a man like Fam," said Nzame, "the same legs and arms, but we shall turn his head and he shall see death."

This was the second man and father of all. Nzame called him Sekume, but did not want to leave him alone, and said, "Make yourself a woman from the tree."

Sekume made himself a woman and she walked and he called her Mbongwe.

When Nzame made Sekume and Mbongwe he made them in two parts, an outer part called Gnoul, the body, and the other which lives in the body, called Nsissim. It is Nsissim who makes Gnoul live. Nsissim goes away when a man dies, but Nsissim does not die. Do you know where he lives? He lives in the eye. The little shining point you see in the middle, that is Nsissim.

Stars above
Fire below
Coal in the hearth
The soul in the eye
Cloud smoke and death.

Sekume and Mbongwe lived happily on earth and had many children. But Fam, the first man,

was imprisoned by God under the earth. With a large stone he blocked the entrance. But the malicious Fam tunnelled at the earth for a long time, and one day, at last he was outside!

Who had taken his place? The new man. Fam was furious with him. Now he hides in the forest to kill them, under the water to capsize their boats.

Remain silent
Fam is listening,
To bring misfortune;
Remain silent.

A Fang story from Gabon

---

1 What similarities can you see in the two stories?
2 What do you think are the important differences in the stories?

The Garden of Eden

1 Why do you think Yahweh was so angry with Adam and Eve?
2 Who do you think was really responsible for their sin?
3 What things were special about the Garden of Eden?
4 What rule did Yahweh give Adam for living in the garden? What did God say would happen if Adam disobeyed?
5 How did the snake persuade Eve that it would be a good idea to eat from the forbidden tree?
6 What happened after Eve ate the apple?
7 How did Adam and Eve react when they heard Yahweh coming and when he spoke to them?
8 Work out all the punishments Yahweh gave to the snake, Adam, Eve and their descendants.

The Revolt against God

1 Why did Nzame decide to punish Fam?
2 How did Nzame punish Fam?
3 Explain carefully what became of Fam, and what he is today.
4 What is the "hard black stone which breaks; throw it into the fire and it burns. . ." How was it made?
5 How did Nzame create life a second time?
6 The new man Nzame made was called Sekume. How were Sekume and Fam different?

Other things to do

A Perfect World

"*The Big Rock Candy Mountain*" was a world perfect for a hobo. What would be a perfect world for — your best friend — your teacher — a relative of yours? Think about how different people would like the world to be.

Describe a world perfect for somebody else, or for several very different people.

Inventions

"*The Boomerang*" story described how a weapon was accidentally invented.

Can you think out an amusing way in which something first came about? What about a corkscrew? A pencil sharpener? A loudspeaker?

You could write the explanation as an ordinary story, or as an aboriginal picture story.

You might prefer to make up some completely fresh inventions for your world, or for the future.

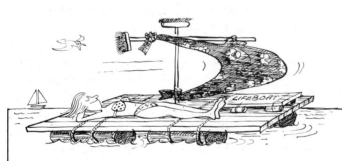

Making Things

Do you do any of these: dressmaking, modelling, gardening, painting?

Have you ever made: a scrapbook, a raft, a sandcastle, a hideout?

Describe carefully a time you made something you were pleased with.

Breaking Rules

Take the list of rules you made for your world. Think about which rules are difficult to keep. Write a story about breaking a rule.

You could write a personal story of how you broke a rule. Or you could imagine the first people breaking God's rule.

The Story of Sun and Moon

Contents

Part 1 How it All Began. Sun Has to Flee
Part 2 Sun Falls in Love . . .
Part 3 . . . and Tackles the Monster
Part 4 Moon is Wicked Again. Justice at Last.
Discussion and Storytelling
Your Writing: Story
The Sun and Moon File

Part I   How it All Began. Sun Has to Flee

Once upon a time the kingdom of the sky was ruled by one great king. He married many wives hoping to get more children, but they all failed to give him any children.

So he divorced all of them except the mother of Moon and Sun. She was a very good mother to her sons, and a good wife to her husband. But life was very hard, for she died when Sun was very young.

The king of the sky looked after his sons and was particularly very fond of Sun, his younger son. Moon was possessive and very jealous of his brother. He always treated Sun unkindly.

When their father was about to die, he called Sun and Moon to his bedside to say a last goodbye. Then he divided his kingdom into two dukedoms to be governed by his two sons, and he divided his wealth between them.

Because Sun was very young, too young to take such a responsibility as ruling half the sky, Moon was asked by his father to act as Sun's regent until Sun became of age to rule his dukedom.

Moon was also asked to look after the half of the wealth that had to go to Sun, and to find a good wife for Sun when he wanted to marry. According to the custom of the people, Moon would have to pay the bride price or dowry on behalf of Sun.

Moon promised to be kind to Sun and to hand over his dukedom and property when Sun became of age. The king of the sky blessed his sons, and then he died.

After the death of his father Moon forgot his promises. He treated Sun like a servant or beggar.

Whenever Sun wanted something Moon always denied it to him. Moon's wife was also very unkind to Sun.

Moon wanted to keep the kingdom of the sky in one piece. He wanted to be its only ruler.

When Sun wished to marry, he went to ask his brother for cattle, goats, and sheep in order to make an offer to his future father-in-law, but Moon would not give him any.

When Sun became of age and demanded permission to rule his dukedom, Moon refused completely and even said that their father had never intended to divide the kingdom. He said he was the elder son and as such he was the right and only heir. Moon threatened to kill his brother when Sun complained about this injustice.

So Sun had to run away for his safety. He went away and decided never to return. He went a long way from his country into a foreign country where his father had many friends. But he did not tell anyone who he really was, for fear his brother would follow him and kill him.

Remembering your reading

1 Work out and write down **all** the things the king said to Moon and Sun at his last goodbye. What did he give to them? What did Moon promise to do? (You should find seven things.)
2 Make a list of all the ways in which Moon treated Sun badly.

33

Part 2 Sun Falls in Love . . .

Sun went to the homestead of the king of this foreign country. The king had many wives, and many children, all girls.

Sun asked the king to give him a job as a shepherd. He was employed, and he lived within the king's homestead. He worked hard and earned the admiration of everyone in the homestead. He was regarded as one of the family.

He had not been there long before he fell in love with one of the daughters of the homestead. The girl was the favourite child of the king and the king had decided that this girl was to be the heir of his kingdom, and so she would not be allowed to marry anyone who would take her out of the family. So her husband had to be from one of the noble families within the kingdom.

This made things difficult for Sun, who was looked on as a poor shepherd, and whose family was not known by the king. Sun was tempted to tell them who he really was, but he feared the embarrassment of admitting he had told a lie.

He was also afraid that if his brother Moon was asked to confirm that Sun *was* his brother, his position might be worse. Moon might lie about Sun's identity, or order him back home. Sun decided to remain as he was and try to win the king over, as he had done as a shepherd.

Near the king's homestead was a large, beautiful lake. In the middle of the lake there was an island of beautiful feathers. They looked like ostrich feathers. Their colours were as the colours of the rainbow. People used to travel from distant places to come and see these magic feathers in the middle of the lake.

Nobody had ever been anywhere near them. Many great sailors had attempted to row their boats near the feathers and they had all mysteriously perished before reaching them.

The king had consulted many witch-doctors to tell him what sort of animal it was that lived in the middle of the lake. Many witch doctors and priests told the king that the mystery was to do with his family. Some said that the existence of these feathers brought ill spirits to the king's family and that was why he was unable to have any sons by his wives.

The king had offered much money to many good sailors to go to the middle of the lake and bring back some of the feathers. Many had perished in the attempt.

To stop many young men from disturbing his daughter, the king made a condition that the only man who would be allowed to marry his beloved girl, would be the man who succeeded in reaching the beautiful feathers, in the middle of the lake, and bringing some of them to him.

All this time Sun was doing well as a herdsman. The king's daughter continued to like him. She thought that one day she would be able to persuade her father to accept Sun as her husband and also to persuade Sun to live within and carry on the king's family.

Remembering and predicting

Before you read any more of the story, decide how you think the story will go on.

For each of the points below, think of as many possibilities as you can, and decide which one you would like to see happening in the story.

1 What do you think the feathers in the large, beautiful lake could be? Why are they there, do you think?

2 Will Sun marry the king's daughter? What things will he have to do to get the king's consent, and how will he manage to do them?

3 Will Sun get his dukedom back? How?

4 In a happy ending, what will happen to Sun/his wife/Moon? In a sad ending, what will happen to them? What do you want to happen?

Part 3   ....and Tackles the Monster

One day Sun decided to go to the lake and find out what animal bore the beautiful magical feathers that floated on the surface of the lake. He realised that it must be a great sea monster. Instead of sailing, or rowing a boat, he decided to swim under the water and take the animal by surprise.

The king's daughter refused to agree to Sun's plan, because she loved him dearly and did not want him to be eaten up by the great monster. But Sun persisted and said he knew how to kill the animal and that he was going to succeed. He told her that he was deeply in love with her and could not wait any more. He would rather die in his attempt to kill the monster than live in such misery. He was sure he was going to be safe and would return to marry her at once.

Sun and the king's daughter went to the mother to tell her of their love. She in turn told the king, who was dismayed at the news. But as he knew that the sea monster was unconquerable, he gave his word that if Sun would bring the feathers from the middle of the lake he would be allowed to marry his favourite daughter.

Sun was very pleased. He prepared a long strong rope made of leather wound round a hollow tube. The rope was miles long. He asked the king to give him the best sword and spear in the homestead. Sun went to a good witch doctor to get magic medicines with which to stupefy the sea monster, and also some poison to kill it with. He poisoned his sword and spear, and when he was ready, Sun asked the daughter of the king to promise that she would stay on the shore and hold the rope while he swam towards the monster. She promised to do this.

Now that all the preparations were ready, Sun asked the king to summon his neighbours to come to the shore of the lake and witness his venture. It was a fine morning. The people were gathered by the lake. Sun knotted the rope about his waist and put one end of it in his mouth, leaving the other end on the shore to be held by his beloved. This served as a breathing apparatus.

He dived into the water with his spear and sword. He swam for days and nights, and the girl stayed by the shore of the lake uncoiling the rope as Sun swam towards the monster. She prayed to God that Sun might be victorious. Of all the men who had proposed to her she was convinced that Sun was the only one who was really genuinely in love with her.

Even the king himself was beginning to respect Sun. He regretted having insisted on Sun's fetching the feathers. He ordered his daughter to try and call Sun back. He said he was sure Sun was a good man and she would have his permission to marry him.

It was not easy to get Sun back. To pull the rope might endanger Sun's life. There was no means of communication, to convey the news to Sun that he now had the approval of the king and that what he was now doing was no longer necessary.

So Sun swam on.

One day at about noon, the people on the shore of the lake saw the blue water in the middle of the lake turn red. It became a pool of blood. They were seized with great fear. Sun must have been killed they thought for a moment.

The king's daughter fainted, and her mother came to hold the rope, and shook it to find if it were loose the other end. But she could feel some object clinging to the rope. She kept on holding it, while other people were looking after her daughter who was crying for her lover.

All at once the people could see a peculiar movement in the feathers. They thought that the animal was coming to kill them after killing Sun.

When the girl regained consciousness, she was told that the feathers were moving towards the shore, and she held the rope again; she could feel something at the other end. Placing her ear against the end of the rope, she could hear Sun's breath and was sure Sun was safe.

Sun had killed the great monster.

He reached it from behind when it was asleep, with its head above the water. To protect its precious, beautiful feathers, the monster had to keep its head above water most of the time during the day so that it could watch out for any intruders. When Sun got near the monster he approached its neck and with his poisoned spear he killed it at one stroke, by sending the spear straight through its heart.

The monster died instantly, without much struggle. And Sun chopped off the tail with its beautiful feathers and carried it with him towards the shore. He swam back for days and nights, and when the weather was clear he waved to the people ashore. They realised then he had killed the monster. Many people came from near and far. They wanted to witness Sun's victory and to attend the wedding of the king's daughter.

Eventually help was sent to Sun to bring him back but he would not get on a boat. He wanted to finish his work the way he planned to do it.

When he stepped ashore he was greeted by his beloved. Yet before he had a moment to say anything, the people were amazed by the sight of cows emerging from the lake. The cows came out in great numbers. They came out in so great a number that people who were counting them could not count any more. Their eyes were tired.

Then out came the bulls, as many as the cows.

Then came the calves, as many as the cows.

Then came goats, as many as the cows and the bulls. Then out came sheep, as many as the cows, bulls, calves and goats. The whole place was drowned with the noise of these herds of cattle, goats and sheep. They were so many that no kingdom had such large herds.

The king was very happy and proud of Sun. He had conquered the great monster that had killed so many people. The herds of cattle, goats and sheep were those the monster had stolen from the kingdom over the years, and had magically lived in its stomach.

The feathers of the great monster were used to thatch the king's houses within the homestead. Some were spread to thatch the new home of the bride and bridegroom.

At this stage Sun told everybody who he really was, and told them he wished to return to his own country and claim his dukedom from his brother Moon. The king was overjoyed to hear this, as the father of Sun had been a great friend of the king, before he died.

Preparations were made to wed Sun to the king's daughter and to escort them to Sun's home.

Remembering your reading

1 Think out and write down all the reasons why Sun decided he would have to tackle the monster.
2 Make a list of the equipment Sun took with him to tackle the monster.
3 Draw a picture of the monster.

Part 4   Moon is Wicked Again. Justice at Last

When Sun reached home with his bride, the beautiful feathers, and a large herd of cattle, goats and sheep, his brother was very surprised. He felt very jealous, for Sun now was many times richer than Moon. Sun's wife was prettier than Moon's wife.

But Sun was very kind and gentle. He forgave his brother and gave him some of the feathers to thatch his house.

Moon could not accept his brother. Although he accepted the gifts given to him by Sun, he was still jealous and thought of doing his brother more harm.

One day, while they were grazing their animals, Moon planned to kill Sun. He asked Sun to go down a salty clay mine and dig some salty clay for their animals. While Sun was in the mine Moon buried him alive and returned home alone with the animals. He told Sun's wife that her husband had had an accident at the mines and was buried there.

She was very sad. She went to the mine to try to dig her husband out, but it was too late. He was dead. She went back to her father with this sad news. Her mother comforted her and promised that she was going to do something about it.

The mother went to a famous witch doctor who was said to be able to bring back the dead. She learnt all the magic of reviving the dead and came back to her daughter. She instructed her to go to the mine and cut bits of flesh from every part of Sun's body and put them in a clean calabash and take them back home to her house.

When she got home she was to hide the calabash somewhere in the house and she was to put some fat and minced meat into the calabash regularly until all the bits of flesh in the calabash were made into a small body by magic. Then Sun's wife would break the calabash and hide the small body somewhere else in the house and continue to feed it with delicate foods, particularly milk and meat.

She fed the small body with delicacies, as she was advised by her mother, and gradually Sun's body was magically transformed from his dead body way off in the mines into the new body in his house.

By the time the mourning days for Sun's death were over, Sun was complete and back in his house in exactly the same form and shape as before.

According to custom, Moon would have to go to the house of Sun's wife at the end of the mourning and stay in the house with her as his bride.

For this occasion Moon had organised a big feast and had invited many people from near and far, including Mrs. Sun's family, to come to witness Moon's new wedding. Of course, Sun and his wife and her family knew what had happened and what was going to happen on the day proposed for the wedding of Sun's wife to Moon.

It was arranged that Sun would come out again on that day, and that he would accuse Moon in the presence of all the people. They would then try Moon and a decision would be reached so that Moon should cease troubling his brother in future.

Sun was sent the most magnificent robes, spear, sword and an elder's staff for the occasion.

When the people were congregated in the royal homestead and all the guests were waiting for the ceremony, the father of Sun's wife stood up and called for the attention of the people. The place at once became silent. One could even hear the noise of a fly flapping its small wings. This was the first time a ruler of a foreign kingdom had stood before them to speak. The king said that before making any speech, he would ask his daughter to come out of the house first. At this point he called her by name and asked her to come out.

To everybody's surprise she came out followed by Sun holding her hand. This was like a dream to many people who had been led to believe that Sun

was dead, and a great horror to Moon who was so guilty of his crimes: expelling his brother from home, depriving him of his heritage, and killing him when he returned.

Moon collapsed from shock and it was hours before he recovered. While he was recovering from the shock people were shouting, asking Sun to kill Moon with his spear.

"Kill him! Kill him, Sun!" they cried, "He is an evil man, kill him!"

"Calm, please be calm," Sun pleaded, "I do not believe in revenge. I shall ask you first to listen to what I have to say and then I shall expect you to make your own judgment."

"Let us hear," they shouted. "What happened?"

Sun told the whole story, from their father's death, and the will, his banishment, and how he was murdered and magically revived by his wife.

The people were satisfied that Moon was an evil man and all agreed that he should be banished far away into the sky and that he should live by night while Sun ruled and lived by day.

That is why the moon is seen at night and sun during the day.

from *Agikuyu Folk Tales* by Ngumbu Njururi

Remembering your reading

1 Work out carefully and write down everything Sun's wife had to do to bring him back to life again.
2 Did the story end as you expected?

Discussion and Storytelling

This story is a very old one. It would be handed down from generation to generation by parents who would tell it to their children to explain why there is day and night. People always ask of a story — is it true? Do you think this story is "true"?

Think about each of the following parts of the story. Do they remind you of other stories? Or happenings in real life? See how many stories you can tell each other when discussing these points:

How Moon treated his brother Sun
Why did Moon treat his brother so badly? Did he have any good reason for doing this? Or was he a bad character?

Think about things you have heard of, in other stories, in the news, in real life where people have treated each other cruelly.

How Sun had to kill the monster to marry the king's daughter
Why did Sun have to do this? Was this right? Should people be able to marry whomever they like? What is your favourite story of lovers who have to overcome great odds in order to be together?

The monster
What was it? Why was it there? Do you think the king and the villagers were responsible for it in any way? What happened when it was killed? Why hadn't someone killed the monster before?

The coming to life again of Sun
Try to think of all the stories you know in which someone is brought to life again.

Sun's treatment of Moon at the end
Sun says he does not believe in revenge. Do you agree with him? Is it easier, or better, to forgive or to take revenge? Try to think of other stories, or things in real life where people have shown forgiveness or taken revenge.

Your Writing: Story

☆ Tell in your own words one of the stories you have thought about when discussing "*The Story of Sun and Moon*".
☆ Write as if you were someone who has suffered a great wrong, as Sun did, but who also manages to get justice in the end.
☆ Imagine that your child asked you a difficult question, like:
   Why do birds fly?
   Why do the stars shine?
   Why does the sea come and go?
   What story could you tell your child which would answer the question and which a child would enjoy listening to?

Other things to do

Suppose people are really determined to find out if there was any truth at all in this story. They journey to the place where people often tell the story. After much searching they come across scraps of papers and documents which suggest that something like the story did happen. See how many of these ideas you can use to make up "*The Sun and Moon File*".

The King of the Sky's Will

One of the documents looks like the will that the king of the sky left.

It starts:

"I, the King of the Sky, being of sound mind, do hereby set down my last will and testament.
1. I do leave....."

and it ends:

"In witness whereof, I sign this day....."

Look back to your answers to question 1, page 33. Use these answers to help you write the will.

The Trial of Moon

All that is found is one paper which gives details of all the things Moon was charged with.

Sun's Diary

Some pages are found which make it seem as if Sun kept a diary. Write out some pages of his diaries.
The times you might write about are:

1   As he decides to leave his home. (Your answer to Part 1 question 2 will help you.)
2   As he decides he must kill the monster. (Your answer to Part 3 question 2 will help you.)
3   After he has killed the monster.
4   After the story is all over.

The Witch Doctor's Potion

The investigator finds the detailed instructions that the witch doctor gave to Sun's wife to make Sun come to life again. Look back to your answer to question 1 on the opposite page. Try and write out the things she had to do in a way which makes it sound like a magical potion.

A Picture of the Monster

Can you make your drawing look old, tattered and faded?

Eye Witness Account of the Killing of the Monster

Luckily the investigator stumbles across a piece of paper on which someone unknown has written down what they saw of the killing of the monster.

Animals

Contents

Five Animal Poems
    Your Writing: Poems
    Making a Radio Programme

Cruel or Kind?
    The Meadow Mouse
    To See the Rabbit
    Discussion
    Your Writing: Opinions

Other things to do
    Animal Alphabet
    Shape Poems
    How the Leopard Got its Spots

Read the poems and look at the pictures. Try reading the poems aloud. Talk about the questions. They will help you to think of ideas for your own poems and show you how to go about writing them.

The Eagle

I am king of the earth,
I am king of the air,
I am king of the ocean.
Everything is around my throne
Under my powerful wings.
Sunrise to sunset
I look over the world
As a tiny coconut fruit
Floating on a silvery sea.
I know the spirit of the air,
I know the spirit of the earth,
I know the spirit of the ocean.
Everything is beneath my wings
Under my powerful tail.

George Tuke

1 Why do you think the eagle feels like a king?
2 What does the world seem like to the eagle?
3 How many times does the writer repeat a word or phrase? Why?
4 What other animals, do you think, might think of themselves as "king"?
5 What other animals might think of themselves as people? Which animal might think of itself as a cleaner? a builder? a musician?

Elephant

Elephant, a spirit in the bush,
Elephant who brings death.
He swallows a whole palmfruit
thorns and all.
He tramples down the grass
with his mortar legs.
Wherever he walks
the grass is forbidden to stand up again.
He tears a man like an old rug
and hangs him up in the tree.
With his single hand
he pulls two palm trees to the ground.
If he had two hands
he would tear the Heaven to shreds.
An elephant is not a load for an old man —
nor for a young man either.

1 How would you describe the attitude the writer has towards the elephant? Love? Admiration? Fear? Awe? Respect? Distrust?
2 Of all the things the writer says the elephant does, which do you find the most remarkable?
3 Of all the things the writer says about the elephant, which do you think is written in the most interesting way?
4 Are there any animals which make you feel respect or awe?

Leopard

Gentle hunter
his tail plays on the ground
while he crushes the skull.

Beautiful death
who puts on a spotted robe
when he goes to his victim.

Playful killer
whose loving embrace
splits the antelope's heart.

1 What's special about the way the writer has described the leopard in the first line of each verse?
2 Can you think of other animals which seem to have "opposite qualities"?

The Snake Song

Neither legs or arms have I
But I crawl on my belly
And I have
Venom, venom, venom!

Neither horns nor hoofs have I
But I spit with my tongue
And I have
Venom, venom, venon!

Neither bows nor guns have I
But I flash fast with my tongue
And I have
Venom, venom, venom!

Neither radar nor missiles have I
But I stare with my eyes
And I have
Venom, venom, venom!

I master every movement
For I jump, run and swim
and I spit
Venom, venom, venom!

John Mbiti

A Spider's Web

A span of silver coins
    delicately laid
Like hanging jewels from
    a curtain of gems.
A fan of petals . . . a pattern
    of lace.

Caroline Benedetti

1 When do you think the writer was looking at a spider's web?

2 What other animals make or build something?

3 What animals do you think are particularly beautiful?

4 This writer has described the spider's web by comparing the web to other things — coins, jewels, gems, patterns, lace.

Make sure you really know what the writer means. What are: the "silver coins", the "hanging jewels from a curtain of gems"? Why does the web look like "a fan of petals . . . a pattern of lace"?

5 Take an animal that you think beautiful. Describe it by comparing it to other things. See if other people can guess which animal you're talking about.
For example, what animal do you think this is:
    a zebra crossing,
    black paths across delicate films,
    a sword of fire?

1 What are all the different ways that a snake can protect and defend itself?

2 Can you see how each verse is written in the same way?

3 Think about other animals and the way they protect and defend themselves. Could you write: "*The Hedgehog Song*", "*The Chameleon Song*", "*The Crab Song*"?

Your Writing: Poems

Planning
☆ Choose the best idea you talked about when you were discussing the poems.
Look again at the poem that gave you the idea to remind yourself how it was written.

or

☆ Write about an animal you know well, or an animal you like or one of the animals in the pictures. Think about the animal's movements, looks, behaviour, and personality.

Drafting
Try it out. Remember that the poems you read were quite short, and didn't rhyme, but the lines were arranged in a pattern. Use one of these patterns, or jot down ideas as they come to you, using one line for each idea.

Revising
Read your poem and make changes to improve it. Ask yourself these questions:
1 Can you improve the words you have used?
2 Are the ideas in the best order?
3 Do the lines stop and start in the best places?
4 Do you want to divide your lines into verses?
5 Can you get a pattern in your poem by making the shape of each verse the same or by repeating something?
6 Give your poem to other people to read. Can they suggest any improvements?

Proofreading
Search for any mistakes you made because you were working quickly.

Presentation
Write out clearly your revised version.

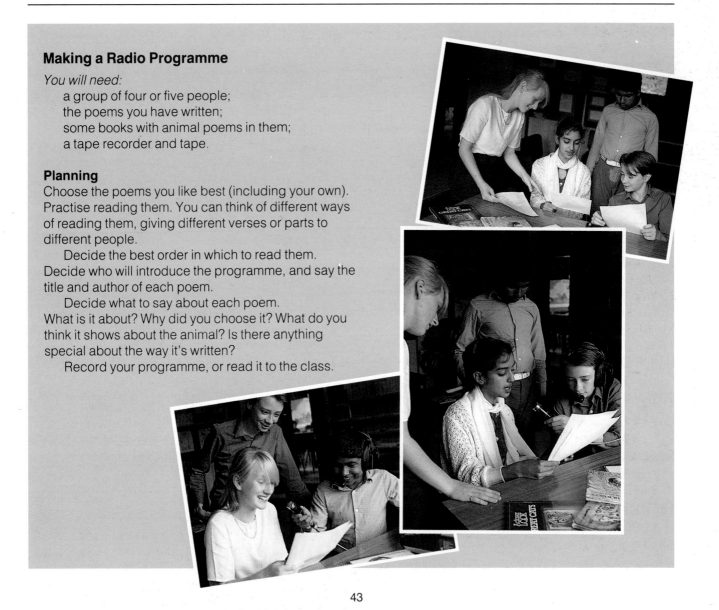

Making a Radio Programme

You will need:
    a group of four or five people;
    the poems you have written;
    some books with animal poems in them;
    a tape recorder and tape.

Planning
Choose the poems you like best (including your own). Practise reading them. You can think of different ways of reading them, giving different verses or parts to different people.
    Decide the best order in which to read them. Decide who will introduce the programme, and say the title and author of each poem.
    Decide what to say about each poem. What is it about? Why did you choose it? What do you think it shows about the animal? Is there anything special about the way it's written?
    Record your programme, or read it to the class.

Cruel or Kind?

In your next piece of writing you will be giving your opinion about the ways that human beings treat animals. Do people treat animals cruelly or kindly? What do you think?

To help you make up your mind, here are two poems to read and some questions to discuss.

The Meadow Mouse

In a shoe box stuffed in an old nylon stocking
Sleeps the baby mouse I found in the meadow,
Where he trembled and shook beneath a stick
Till I caught him up by the tail and brought him in,
Cradled in my hand,
A little quaker, the whole body of him trembling,
His absurd whiskers sticking out like a cartoon-
	mouse,
His feet like small leaves,
Little lizard-feet,
Whitish and spread wide when he tried to struggle
	away,
Wriggling like a miniscule puppy.

Now he's eaten his three kinds of cheese and drunk
	from his bottle-cap watering-trough —
So much he just lies in one corner,
His tail curled under him, his belly big
As his head; his bat-like ears
Twitching, tilting towards the least sound.

Do I imagine he no longer trembles
When I come close to him?
He seems no longer to tremble.

But this morning the shoe-box house on the back
	porch is empty.
Where has he gone, my meadow mouse,
My thumb of a child that nuzzled in my palm?
To run under the hawk's wing,
Under the eye of the great owl watching from the
	elm-tree,
To live by courtesy of the shrike, the snake, the
	tom-cat.

I think of the nestling fallen into the deep grass,
The turtle gasping in the dusty rubble of the
	highway,
The paralytic stunned in the tub, and the water
	rising, —
All things innocent, hapless, forsaken.

Theodore Roethke

1 (1st verse) How and where did the boy catch the mouse?
   What sort of home did he make for the mouse?
2 (2nd verse) Why do you think the mouse's ears are twitching, listening for the least sound?
3 (3rd verse) Why does the boy hope the mouse will stop trembling?
4 (4th verse) Where has the meadow mouse gone?
   What dangers will he face in the country?
   Why do you think the mouse has left the boy?
5 (last verse) In the last verse, the writer says that the meadow mouse makes him think of different animals and people.
   What are the three animals and people he thinks of?
   Why does he think of them?
6 Have you ever tried to keep a wild or stray animal?
   Do you think that people should keep wild or stray animals?

44

To See the Rabbit

We are going to see the rabbit.
We are going to see the rabbit.
Which rabbit, people say?
Which rabbit, ask the children?
The only rabbit,
The only rabbit in England,
Sitting behind a barbed-wire fence
Under the floodlights, neon lights,
Sodium lights,
Nibbling grass
On the only patch of grass
in England, in England
(Except the grass by the hoardings
Which doesn't count)
We are going to see the rabbit
And we must be there on time.

First we shall go by escalator
Then we shall go by underground,
And then we shall go by motorway,
And then by helicopterway,
And the last ten yards we shall have to go
On foot.

And now we are going
All the way to see the rabbit
We are nearly there,
We are longing to see it
And so is the crowd
Which is here in thousands
With mounted policemen
And big loudspeakers
And bands and banners
And everyone has come a long way.

But soon we shall see it
Sitting and nibbling
The blades of grass
In — but something has gone wrong!
Why is everyone so angry
Why is everyone so jostling
And slanging and complaining?

The rabbit has gone,
Yes, the rabbit has gone,
He has actually burrowed down into the earth
And made himself a warren under the earth,
Despite all these people,
And what shall we do?
What *can* we do?

It is all a pity, you must be disappointed.
Go home and do something else for today.
Go home again, go home for today.
For you cannot hear the rabbit under the earth
Remarking rather sadly to himself,
As he rests in his warren, under the earth:
"It won't be long, they are bound to come,
They are bound to come and find me, even here."

Alan Brownjohn

1 (1st verse) Why are the people so excited at going
   to see a rabbit?
   Describe the place where the rabbit is kept.
   Why is it like this?
   Why do you think there is only one rabbit left?
   What is the rabbit eating?
   What do you think has happened to the rest of the
   grass in England?
2 (2nd verse) What means of transport do the people
   use to get to the rabbit?
   Do you think the people are used to walking?
   Give your reason.
3 (3rd verse) When the people get to where the
   rabbit is kept, what are the first things they see?
   Why do you think there are mounted policemen
   there?
   Why are the people angry and disappointed?
   (Think of at least two reasons.)
4 Why has the rabbit dug a hole? (Think very
   carefully about this, and suggest as many reasons
   as you can.)
5 When do you think this poem is happening — in
   the past, now, or in the future? Give your reasons
   for what you say.

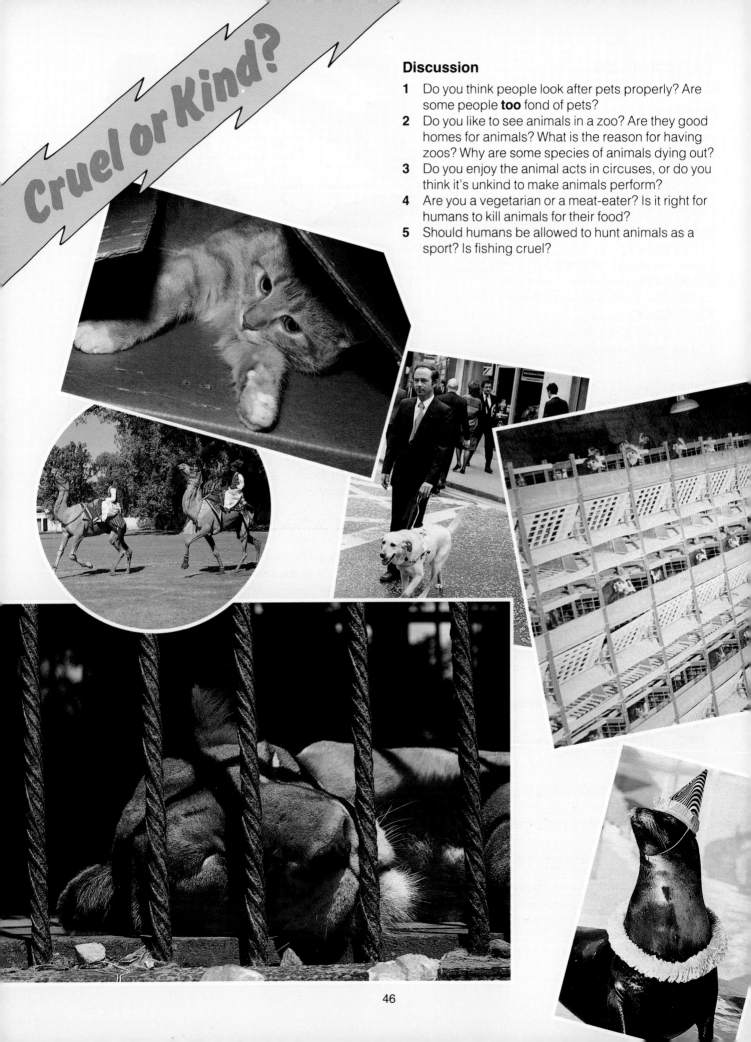

Cruel or Kind?

Discussion

1 Do you think people look after pets properly? Are some people **too** fond of pets?
2 Do you like to see animals in a zoo? Are they good homes for animals? What is the reason for having zoos? Why are some species of animals dying out?
3 Do you enjoy the animal acts in circuses, or do you think it's unkind to make animals perform?
4 Are you a vegetarian or a meat-eater? Is it right for humans to kill animals for their food?
5 Should humans be allowed to hunt animals as a sport? Is fishing cruel?

Your Writing: Opinions

Are human beings cruel or kind to animals?

Planning

Decide what you think at the moment.
Which of these will you do in your essay?

a) Persuade someone that human beings are cruel to animals?

b) Persuade someone that human beings are kind to animals?

c) Explain that human beings are cruel in some ways, and kind in others?

d) Work out your opinions as you go along because you're not sure yet?

Decide which of these topics you can write something about:

> Pets
> Circuses
> Blood sports and fishing
> Animals at work
> Animals as food
> Zoos
> Animals in experiments

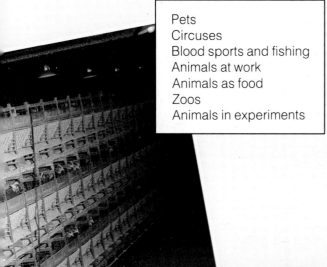

Drafting

Write as much as you can in answer to the question:
Are human beings cruel or kind to animals?

Revising

Making a good start   Start off with a short paragraph, an introduction, explaining to your reader what you are going to do in your essay. Which point of view have you decided on: **a**, **b**, **c**, or **d**? Which of the topics above are you going to write about?

Making it more detailed   If you haven't written very much, you could plan paragraphs to add to your writing. For example, suppose you think that people are kind to circus animals in some ways, and cruel in other ways. Jot down some points about each, like this:

> ## CIRCUSES
>
> *KIND*
> animals well fed, well looked after
> good medical attention
> they learn a skill
> seem to enjoy their work
> enjoy a close relationship with human beings
> often get a good place to go to in their old age
>
> *CRUEL*
> they are caged in
> they do unnatural tricks.
> they look undignified so people laugh at them
> they are trained harshly, with whips

Finishing off   Round off your essay with another short paragraph, a conclusion, giving your final answer and any ideas about what should be done.

If your introduction said . . .	your conclusion might say . . .
Human beings are cruel to animals.	How can we stop this?
Human beings are kind to animals.	How can we make sure they keep on being kind?
Human beings are kind in some ways, cruel in other ways.	Do you now think there are more points on one side?
I'm not sure yet.	What do you now think the answer is, and why?

Use pages 16 and 17 to help you proofread and present your writing clearly.

Other things to do

Animal Alphabet

Mr Noah stood at the top of the gangway with a loudhailer made from a buffalo horn: "Aardvark!" he called, "addax, ai anoa, anteater, armadillo . . .

Can you make an animal alphabet?
Armadillo
Buffalo
Cheetah
Dingo . . .

Shape Poems

Look at this famous poem from "*Alice in Wonderland*".

'It *is* a long tail, certainly,' said Alice, looking down with wonder at the Mouse's tail; 'but why do you call it sad?' And she kept on puzzling about it while the Mouse was speaking, so that her idea of the tale was something like this:——

'Fury said to
a mouse, That
he met in the
house, "Let
us both go
to law: *I*
will prose-
cute *you*.—
Come, I'll
take no de-
nial: We
must have
the trial;
For really
this morn-
ing I've
nothing
to do."
Said the
mouse to
the cur,
"Such a
trial, dear
sir, With
no jury
or judge,
would
be wast-
ing our
breath."
"I'll be
judge,
I'll be
jury,"
said
cun-
ning
old
Fury:
"I'll
try
the
whole
cause,
and
con-
demn
you to
death."

As you can see the words of the poem form the shape of a mouse's tail.
Make up some poems in this way. The easiest way to do it is to:
Draw the shape of the animal in pencil first.
Then write your chosen words — describing the animal — or what the animal might say — in and around the shape, in ink.
Finally rub out the pencil drawing.

Can you make more than one list?
Can you make a bird alphabet?
an insect alphabet?
a fish alphabet?

48

How the Leopard Got its Spots

One day ant's mother died and all the animals decided to accompany him to the funeral which was at some distance from their village.

As they went along the road from the village they passed a garden-egg farm, a farm full of wonderful, ripe garden-eggs. Now the leopard was particularly fond of garden-eggs, indeed he doted on them. His mouth watered when he saw them and as he passed the farm he went slower and slower until he was the last animal in the procession. Then he sat down in the path and thought. Soon he was alone. He looked carefully round and seeing no-one he whipped round and rushed into the farm.

He ate and he ate and he ate, until nearly half the farm had been consumed. Then he could eat no more and went off slowly along the path to join the other animals.

As luck would have it, the farmer arrived just after he left and, seeing all the animals passing along the road, ran after them and began to curse and swear at them for having stolen his food. Of course, the animals denied having stolen the garden-eggs and many were indignant at the accusations. They stopped to argue and the farmer demanded that they should stand trial. This they willingly agreed to do — provided it did not take too long or they would be late for the funeral.

The farmer quickly made a great fire in a hollow in the ground and told the animals to jump over it. "If you are innocent," he said, "you will not be harmed, but the guilty one will fall into the fire."

One after another the animals leapt over the flame, some of them singing a song to get up their courage before they jumped. At last only the leopard was left. Everyone expected him to cross the smouldering embers easily. He sang one song. He started another; the animals were impatient to go on to the funeral and shouted at him to hurry. He got ready to spring but — maybe it was the garden-eggs in his stomach, maybe it was his nerves. The animals saw him leap into the air, but instead of coming down on the other side he fell into the middle of the smouldering embers. He howled and rushed from the fire rolling on the ground, but the fire had burnt patches in his fur, some black and some brown. The animals stared in amazement and then scolded the leopard as a thief. The farmer felt he had had enough punishment and left him alone to crawl back home, shamed before all the others.

And so to this day the leopard carries a spotted coat, a perpetual reminder of his greed.

from *Tales of an Ashanti Father* by Peggy Appiah

Your Writing

Write your own story about an animal, explaining how it became the way it is now. Use one of these titles or make up one of your own.
☆ How the Tiger Got its Stripes
☆ Why Giraffes Have long Necks
☆ How the Elephant Got its Trunk
☆ Why Whales Live in the Sea
☆ Why Ants Are So Small

Stories from the Ramayana

Contents

The Kidnap of Sita
    Notes about the Characters
    Making a Display
    Performing the Story

Hanuman
    Writing about Hanuman

Other things to do
    Stories
    A Cartoon Strip
    Reading

"*The Ramayana*", a great book of India, tells the adventures of Rama, the Prince of Ayodhya, and his wife Sita.

This first story takes place when Rama is living in the forest with Sita and his brother Lakshman. They journey through the forest doing good and destroying evil wherever they find it.

One day Rama and Lakshman defeat the she-demon Surpnakha, who had wanted Rama for herself, and cut off her ears and nose. But Surpnakha is sister of the dreaded Ravana, king of Sri Lanka. She goes to him for help. . .

The Kidnap of Sita

Ravana, the ten-headed king of Sri Lanka, was feared by gods and demons alike. Long ago, he had been a great worshipper of the gods and the god Brahma, pleased with him, offered him anything he wanted. Ravana had asked that no god or demon should ever defeat him. Ravana had not thought it necessary to include humans in his list. He did not think they had a chance of defeating him anyway. He was a demon king and he scorned humans. This then was the mighty Ravana who had never known defeat.

When Surpnakha stormed into the presence of her brother, Ravana was shocked to see her disfigured face. "Who has dared to do such a thing to you?" he asked her.

Surpnakha stamped her big feet in anger and said, "The banished princes of Ayodhya. They have not only dared to cut off my ears and nose but have also killed your brothers, Khar and Dushan, who went to punish them for the insult done to me. Surely you will not allow such a grave disgrace to remain unavenged. You must destroy these princes. Moreover," she added slyly, "Sita, the wife of Rama, is very beautiful. She would make a lovely queen for you, dear brother."

Of course, Ravana would punish these princes. But that was not all. When he heard of Sita's beauty, he decided to carry her away. He would bring her to Lanka and marry her. If he did this

then Rama would be well punished for daring to insult the sister of the mighty Ravana.

The demon-king was so proud of the power given him by the gods that he had no doubt in his mind that he would defeat the princes in battle and then take Sita by force. But then he thought of what had happened to his brothers and he decided to carry away Sita by trickery and deceit.

So Ravana summoned his chariot and flew away at great speed. Over the ocean he flew and over the hills and forests till he came to the den of Mareech, the magician.

Now, this Mareech was a very cunning fellow, and could turn himself into any man or bird or beast at will, by the aid of magic. Ravana stopped his chariot outside Mareech's den and said, "Mareech, my sister has been insulted by the princes of Ayodhya. They have also killed my brothers, Khar and Dushan. I wish to avenge all this by kidnapping Sita. Change yourself into a golden deer and walk near their hut. You lure Rama away from there and I will do the rest."

"Rama will surely kill me," said the frightened Mareech.

"In that case," said Ravana, "before you die, imitate the voice of Rama and call out to Lakshman for help!" The frightened Mareech dared not disobey. Turning himself into a golden deer, he appeared before the hut of Rama. Sita was enchanted when she saw the wonderful animal. Pointing to it, she said to Rama, "My Lord, I wish to have that deer. Is it not beautiful?"

"It is too beautiful to be true," thought Lakshman. So he said to Rama, "I think that is not an ordinary animal. Have you ever seen a golden deer before? I am sure it is a demon in disguise. Do not try to go after it."

But Rama would not listen. He picked up his bow and his quiver of arrows and said, "As Sita wants the deer, I must get it for her. You, Lakshman, must guard her while I am away. On no account must you leave her alone in this forest."

As soon as Rama gave chase, the deer ran swiftly through the forest. Little by little it led Rama far away from the hut. Rama had come a long way off when he realised that he could not take the deer alive. So he shot it with his arrow but before it fell, it turned back into Mareech. Then Rama remembered the warning of Lakshman and felt uneasy. The demon imitated the voice of Rama and wailed, "Lakshman, brother Lakshman, help me!" Rama was now frightened. He knew now that he had been fooled. But why? For what purpose? Was Sita safe? Hastily, he retraced his steps towards the hut.

In the meantime, when Sita heard the call of Rama, she cried, "Brother Lakshman, go immediately to my Lord's help. I am sure he is in trouble."

"I do not believe that Rama is in trouble," replied Lakshman. "It must be some trick of the demons. Moreover, I cannot leave you alone in this forest. Such are the commands of brother Rama."

His words made Sita very angry. She spoke harshly to him and said, "You do not seem at all worried about my Lord. Is it because he is your step-brother? Go, or I shall kill myself."

Lakshman felt helpless. He had never disobeyed his brother. What was he to do, for he could not disregard Sita's commands either. So, very much against his wishes, he decided to go. But before he went, he took a stick, drew a circle around the entrance of the hut, and said, "Do not, on any account, step beyond this charmed circle and no harm will come to you."

Ravana was hiding behind a tree. He had heard and seen everything that had happened. He was pleased to see that his plan was working out so well. As soon as Lakshman went after Rama, Ravana quickly changed himself into an aged holy man.

With a begging bowl in one hand he approached the hut. Holy men were always welcome to Rama's hut and when Sita saw one at the door, she welcomed him and offered him fruits. But Ravana shook his head. He knew that he could not kidnap Sita as long as she was inside the charmed circle. He must make her come out of it.

So he said, "I am a holy man and as such cannot enter any home. I cannot accept your offer of fruits from inside the hut. If you want me to accept your offerings, you will have to come out and give them to me."

What was Sita to do? How could she send a holy man away? That would displease Rama. What harm could an old holy man do? So, disregarding Lakshman's warning, she stepped across the charmed line, fruits in hand.

The moment she did this, Ravana sprang on her like a tiger on its prey and seized her. Sita was terrified. She cried and struggled hard but in vain. Ravana was merciless and too strong for her. He carried the crying Sita to his magic chariot. Soon, it rose to the sky and sped away.

Sita was faint with fear and anger. She cried, "How dare you do this to me, the wife of the great Rama? Rama will surely kill you and destroy your whole family for this treachery. Rama, O Rama, where are you? Save me from this wicked demon. O brother Lakshman, forgive my unkind words and come to my aid."

She wailed loud and long, but who was to give her any answer? The chariot flew on and on through the sky.

adapted from *The Story of Ramayana* by Bani Roy Choudhry

Notes about the Characters

1 Write down the names of all the characters.
2 For each one, think up a motto, a saying or a slogan which sums them up, and their part in the story. For example, what about Surpnakha? What is she like and what does she do in the story? What phrases would sum her up?

REVENGE IS MY SECOND NAME!
RAMA! AT ANY PRICE!
SITA SHALL PAY FOR MY EARS AND NOSE!

3 Now make notes about each character in the story. For example start with Lakshman. Write down quickly all you know about him and what he said and did in the story. Try it on your own first, and then compare your list of points with the one below.

Notes on Lakshman

Brother of Rama.

Always helps him.

Tried to persuade Rama not to go after the golden deer because he thought it was a demon in disguise — failed.

Doesn't believe cry for help is from Rama; doesn't want to leave Sita.

Feels helpless when Sita accuses him of being faithless to Rama, and says she will kill herself if he doesn't go to help Rama.

Draws charmed circle around hut, tells Sita not to step outside it.

A slogan for Lakshman:
IF ONLY THEY'D LISTENED TO ME!
I DID MY BEST!

Making a Display

Use your notes and your slogans to make a display about characters in the story of Sita.
Here's one way of doing it.

Do a drawing of Lakshman, and put the slogan you made up for him underneath in big letters.

Use your list of points to help you write as if you were him speaking and telling what happened in the story. You could start like this:

My name is Lakshman. I am the brother of Rama and I have spent many years with him and his wife Sita in exile, far away from home, helping him in any way I could.

I thought there would be trouble after we had cut off the ears and nose of the she-devil Surpnakha, And I was right! One day Sita saw a....

Put your piece of writing underneath the drawing and motto.

Performing the Story

Choose a piece of writing about each character. Choose the best order for them. Read them out.
Here is a list of possible scenes, with some hints about points to emphasise:

1 Surpnakha asks for revenge. (Show why she told Ravana about Sita.)
2 Ravana and Mareech make the plan. (Why did Ravana need help? Mareech is a magician, but frightened.)
3 Rama, Sita and Lakshman see the deer. (Is it real or not?)
4 Lakshman, Sita and the charmed circle. (Make the argument between the two a bitter one.)
5 Ravana and Sita. (Will Sita fall for the trick? Will she disobey Lakshman's command?)

When Rama discovered that Sita had been kidnapped, he was distraught. His only thought was to find her and bring her home, but he needed help. Rama knew of only one person who could help, and that was. . .

Hanuman

Hanuman was half man and half monkey, and general of the monkey army. With his magical powers he could shrink to the size of a mosquito, shoot up taller than a pine tree, shorten or lengthen his tail at will, and fly. Hanuman was strong and good, and used his powers to help those who were weak or in danger. He was the devoted friend of Rama and a faithful believer in the gods.

Rama asked Hanuman to find Sita, and gave him a ring to give to her. Then Hanuman set his army of monkeys to look for her. The monkeys searched through the jungles and forests, in fields and on mountains, in tiny villages and great cities. Sita was nowhere to be found.

At last Hanuman and his army came to the southernmost tip of the country, to the edge of the Indian Ocean. There on a cliff top they met the king of the eagles.

"I am looking for the princess Sita," said Hanuman. "Have you seen her?"

"Yes, I have seen her," said the king of the eagles. "Ravana, king of the demons, has taken her prisoner."

"Where has he taken her?" Hanuman asked.

The king of the eagles pointed across the sea with his wing. "Do you see that island on the

horizon? That is Lanka. It is where the demons have built their city, and where Ravana's palace stands. It is surrounded by giants and demons with many heads. Sita is there, and she will never escape."

At this the monkey army lost heart, but in a thunderous voice Hanuman declared that he would cross the ocean and rescue Sita. He knelt down to pray for success and strength. The image of Rama appeared before him and blessed him. Then thanking the king of the eagles, he leapt off the cliff and flew towards the island of Lanka.

In his haste to reach the palace of the demon king, he flew low, skimming across the sea.

The gods on heaven were pleased to see Hanuman's devotion and courage. But they wanted to test him further to see if he was fit to complete his great task. So they sent Surasa, the mother of Snakes, to test him. She took the form of a fierce demoness and stopped him in mid-air. Hanuman folded his hands and said, "Please do not stop me. I am on my way to Lanka to rescue the fair wife of Lord Rama. If you must eat me then please have a little patience. I promise to return to you after I have completed my task."

But the demoness refused to listen and she sprang upon Hanuman. This angered him and he increased his size. To his dismay the mouth of the demoness became even larger. The more he increased his size, the larger grew her mouth. He realised that this was no ordinary demoness. He turned his mind to Rama and immediately knew that she was Surasa, the mother of Snakes. He jumped into her mouth.

Hanuman felt himself sliding down a long tunnel; then he landed in a pool of water in the monster's vast stomach. All around him floated skeletons, broken masts and pieces of sail, the remains of ships the monster had swallowed.

Hanuman blew himself up like a balloon. He grew bigger and bigger, until he almost filled the monster's stomach. Then he began to jump about, poking and prodding at its sides. The monster felt uncomfortable and thrashed around in the sea, making huge waves. Hanuman was flung from side to side of the great dark cave of its stomach.

Suddenly he caught a glimpse of light at the end of the tunnel; the monster had reared up out of the sea and opened its mighty mouth to get some air. Hanuman lost no time. He shrank to his normal size and flew up towards the opening of the tunnel, and before the monster knew what was happening, he had shot out of its mouth and was free.

Surasa was pleased and, taking her own form, blessed him, saying, "You are indeed worthy to seek out Sita. Go your way. May the gods watch over you!"

Now Hanuman sped towards the shores of Lanka. He could see a great wall lining the beach, with hundreds of soldiers guarding it. He knew he could not get past them as he was, so he made himself shrink until he was even smaller than a mosquito, and flew right over the wall.

Within the walls lay the demon city. Giant warriors roamed its streets, carrying spears and clubs. Mighty elephants were lined up ready for war. Hanuman flew through the streets towards the palace, a magnificent building with golden domes and minarets.

It was night time. Guards watched the gates, but inside the palace everyone was asleep. Hanuman flew through room after room, all filled with gold furniture. In one room he saw the demon king's warrior son, Indrajit, sprawled on a great bed. In another room slept an ugly giant, Ravana's brother, who was said to sleep for six months of every year.

In the largest room of all Hanuman saw the demon king. He was lying on an enormous bed, his ten heads next to each other on a long pillow, each one snoring loudly.

Hanuman searched every room, but Sita was nowhere. At last he went out into the garden and there he found her. She was sitting under a tree in a circle of guards. Her beautiful face was sad, and he could see that she had been crying.

Hanuman alighted on the ground beside her, returned to his normal size and softly whispered her name. He told her who he was and how he had come to find her. Sita was distrustful at first.

"How am I to know that you have really come from my lord? You may be one of the demons in disguise," she said.

Hanuman took out Rama's ring and said, "To prove that I have really come from Rama, here is the ring he has sent for you."

Sita's eyes filled with tears as she recognised Rama's ring. She said, "Go back to Rama and tell him of my plight. Tell him that I await his arrival day and night, to rescue me from the demons. Give this jewel from my hair to him."

She also gave Hanuman a juicy fruit to eat. The taste was so delicious that he begged for more. Pointing to the trees, Sita said, "There they grow. Eat to your fill."

Great was his joy as he jumped from tree to tree and plucked the delicious fruits and ate them. The noise awoke the guards who spotted him at once and ran towards him. Their shouts woke Ravana, and he sent his warrior son, Indrajit, out to fight with Hanuman. Indrajit brought his bow and arrow, and shot his arrows at Hanuman. The arrows were snakes, and Hanuman fell to the ground, caught up in their slithering coils.

Then Hanuman let himself be bound and taken to the demon king. Ravana was sitting on his golden throne, his ten heads and twenty arms all shaking with fury.

"You have annoyed me, monkey," said Ravana. "I am going to punish you."

The demon king knew that monkeys are proud of their tails, so he ordered his guards to set fire to Hanuman's. He told them to seize the tail, wrap cloth around it, pour oil on the cloth and set fire to it.

But as the soldiers did so, Hanuman made his tail grow longer and longer, till it trailed outside the door of the throne room. The soldiers ran to and fro, trying to keep hold of the tail and find more cloth to wrap it in and more oil to pour on it.

"Light the tail!" shouted Ravana, his ten heads glaring at the captive. An orange flame shot up from Hanuman's tail, but just then Hanuman

began to shrink. The ropes that bound him slipped to the ground. He stepped out of them and with a roar flew out of the palace, his tail alight.

When Sita saw Hanuman's tail burning she prayed to Agni, the god of fire, to save him. Hanuman realised the flames were doing him no harm, and he began to swish his tail about until the roof caught fire.

Soon the palace was ablaze. Hanuman leapt to the roof of a nearby house and set fire to it, then flew all over the city, setting fire to the houses of the demons. In a few moments the entire city was a mass of flame, with demons running in all directions to escape the fire.

Hanuman swooped down to the sea and dipped his tail in the water to put out the fire. He then soared away from Lanka and back to Rama, to tell him that Sita had been found.

adapted from *The Indian Storybook*, by Rani Singh

Writing about Hanuman

Add Hanuman to the display of characters you made after the first story.

Planning and Notemaking

1 Make a list of the surprising, magic, amazing things you hear about Hanuman.
2 Make a list of all the things that happened to Hanuman while he was away from his army.
3 What do you think made him so strong, fearless and the possessor of magical powers?
   Was it: just luck?
           his personality to be like that?
           his devotion to Rama?
           his belief in the gods?
4 Make up a slogan for Hanuman, and put it underneath a drawing of Hanuman.

Storytelling or Writing

Now use your notes to tell the story that Hanuman would have told his army when he arrived back on the mainland.

Other things to do

Stories

Write down how you imagine Rama finally rescued Sita.

A Cartoon Strip

Write your own story in pictures of a heroine or hero with magical powers. Choose a small part of one of the stories you have read, and present it like a cartoon strip. Use captions and speech bubbles to tell the story.

Reading

Read more about Rama, Sita and Hanuman in either of the two books from which these stories were taken, or in *The Ramayana* by Elizabeth Seeger (Dent) and *A Book of Goblins* ed. Alan Garner (Puffin). *The Indian Storybook* by Rani Singh is published by Heinemann. *The Story of Ramayana* by Bani Roy Choudhry is published by Kemkant Press (New Delhi).

The Story of Harriet Tubman

Contents

Part 1   At Miss Susan's

Part 2   Follow the North Star

Part 3   Night-time, Daytime

Harriet Tubman's Character

Drama

Other things to do

Who Was Harriet Tubman?

More than a hundred years ago, in the year 1820, a baby girl was born. She was born in a small cabin, on a plantation in the state of Maryland. The baby's mother was Old Rit. The baby's father was Ben. They were Negro slaves.

All the slaves on this Maryland plantation belonged to the master, Edward Brodas. The master owned many slaves, and now he owned this baby. Her real name was Araminta. The people on the plantation called her Minty when she was a little girl. They called her Harriet when she was older.

Later she was called by another name. All over the land she was known as Moses. People said she was like Moses of the Bible. When his people were slaves in Egypt, Moses led them out of Egypt. He led them to freedom. And Harriet Tubman — like Moses — led hundreds of slaves to freedom.

Part 1   At Miss Susan's

Harriet could not fall asleep. Underneath the blanket the dirt floor was hard, but she was used to that. Her brothers were talking, but she was used to that, too. It was their words that were keeping her awake. Terrible, scary words.

"They say the master has no more money," one of her brothers said.

"That's why so many of our people are gone," another brother said.

"He sells the slaves to get money. Or he sends them away to work for other plantation owners."

"Who will be next? One of us?"

"Shush. You'll scare the little ones."

Harriet whispered in the dark. "Please, Lord," she prayed. "Don't let the master send my brothers and sisters away. Please Lord."

The next day the air was warm. The sun was golden. It was too nice a day to worry, but Harriet thought of the words she heard in the dark. "Who will be next? One of us?" That same morning a woman came to the plantation to see the master.

"I want a girl to take care of my baby," Miss Susan told Edward Brodas. "I can only pay you a few pennies a week for her."

"I have just the girl for you," Mr. Brodas said. "She's only seven, but she can do the job."

Miss Susan's wagon took Harriet further and further away from the plantation. What would her family say, she wondered? How would they feel when they learned she had been sent away? There had been no time to say goodbye.

Harriet found out right away what work she had to do. Miss Susan told her to dust and sweep. Harriet knew how to sweep, because she had often swept the dirt floor of her own cabin, but she did not know how to dust. She had never learned, for there was no fine furniture in a slave's cabin. Miss Susan whipped her for not knowing the right way to dust.

Every day Harriet cleaned the house and ran errands. Every night Harriet rocked the baby. Harriet had to make sure that the baby did not wake up and cry.

The baby slept in a cradle near Miss Susan's bed. Above the bed was a shelf where Miss Susan kept her whip made of rawhide. If the baby woke up, and began to cry, Miss Susan reached for her whip. Harriet was whipped so often that she had scars on her neck for the rest of her life.

One day she ran away. But she did not know how to get home. Years later Harriet told what happened.

"One morning Miss Susan had the baby, and I stood by the table waiting until I was to take it. Near me was a bowl of sugar lumps. I never had anything good. . . And that sugar, right by me, did look so nice, and my mistress' back was turned to me. So I just put my fingers in the bowl to take one lump, and she turned and saw me. The next minute she had the rawhide down.

"I gave one jump out of the door. I ran and I ran. By and by I came to a great pigpen. There was an old sow there, and eight or ten little pigs. I tumbled over the high part of the fence and fell on the ground.

"And there I stayed from Friday until the next Tuesday fighting with those little pigs for the potato peelings. By Tuesday I was so starved I knew I had to go back to my mistress. I didn't have anywhere else to go, even though I knew what was coming."

By now Harriet was very weak and was not able to do much work. So Miss Susan brought her back to Edward Brodas.

"She wasn't worth six pennies," Miss Susan told him.

Remembering your reading

1   Why was the master getting rid of some slaves?
2   Did Miss Susan buy Harriet?
3   What were Harriet's jobs at Miss Susan's?
4   Why did Harriet go back to Miss Susan, after escaping?
5   Why did Miss Susan take Harriet back to her master? What sort of person was Miss Susan?

Part 2   Follow the North Star

Harriet was growing up. By the time she was eleven years old, she was very strong. She worked from sunrise to sunset. She ploughed the cornfields. She loaded heavy wood on to wagons. She worked as hard as a man, but she was happier than she had ever been, because she loved being out of doors. Out of doors she felt almost free.

Free. Harriet thought of freedom all the time. Many slaves had tried to run away. The ones that were caught were brought back and beaten. Then they were put in chains and sent to plantation owners who lived in states even further South — where it would be harder to escape. There they were put to work on big cotton or rice plantations.

At night many slaves came to Old Rit's cabin. They talked in whispers. They sang softly of the states up North — and beyond. Of a land called Canada. Men could be free up North, they said.

"How do you get there?" Harriet asked.

"By Underground Railroad," they told her.

"Is there really a train that runs underneath the earth?" she asked.

"No," one of the slaves said. "We call it 'underground' because it is secret. There are special secret roads and paths that lead North. There are people who hide runaway slaves and help them on their way. These people hate slavery. They are called 'station masters'. Their houses are called 'stations'."

Harriet listened. Her eyes had a faraway look.

The man said, "The Underground Railroad has 'conductors' too. The conductors are people who come secretly to the South. They lead groups of slaves to freedom. They lead them North — always North. Always following the North Star."

From the door of her cabin, Harriet could see the bright star, shining like a far-off beam of hope in the night sky.

Follow the North Star to freedom.

Some day she would.

"I'm Going to Leave You"

One day, about four years after she was married, Harriet learned that she was going to be sold. She was going to be sent further South to work on a big cotton plantation.

This was the time to escape. This was the time to run away to the North. Harriet remembered the name of a white woman who had once promised to help her. The woman lived in Bucktown, not far away. Her home was a station on the "Underground Railroad". Was the woman still there?

Would she remember Harriet? Harriet decided not to wait another day. Two of her brothers were going to be sold too, and they said they would escape with her.

Harriet could not say goodbye to anyone — not even to her father and her mother. An escape had to be secret. That evening she walked past the slave cabins, and in her low, deep voice she sang:

When that old chariot comes,
I'm going to leave you,
I'm bound for the promised land.
Friends, I'm going to leave you.

Later, after she was gone, her friends and family thought about that song. They knew it was Harriet's good-bye message. They knew that the promised land was the North.

The sky was clear, the North Star was bright when Harriet and her brothers started out. She was glad that her brothers were with her. There was danger ahead. But she did not feel so frightened with them along.

Harriet led the way and they started through the woods. Her brothers jumped at every sound. They were afraid the slave-catchers would be after them — with dogs to track them down. After a little while the brothers stopped. They whispered together. Then they told Harriet they were turning back. They said it was too dangerous and that they would surely be caught. Harriet tried to make them change their mind. Yes, it was dangerous, she said. But wasn't freedom worth the dangers? But they would not go on.

Now Harriet was alone, but she didn't feel alone. She felt that God would take care of her.

"I'm going to hold steady unto You," she prayed. "And You've got to see me through."

All that night she walked through the woods toward Bucktown. She was tired, frightened, and hungry. Was she being followed? Harriet listened for the pounding of horses' hoofs, but the only pounding she heard was the sound of her own frightened heartbeats. She listened for the barking of the slave-catcher's dogs, but she heard only the sounds of the forest — the running brook, the blowing leaves.

At last Harriet came to Bucktown. She found the house of the woman who had promised to help her. The woman remembered her, invited her in and gave her some food. She told Harriet where to go next, and how to find the next "station" on the "Underground Railroad".

Harriet was travelling the Underground Railroad at last. Travelling North to freedom.

By day she hid. She slept wherever she could. One day she hid in an attic. Another day she hid in a pile of potatoes under a cabin floor.

By night she moved North. One night she travelled in the bottom of a farmer's wagon. She hid under a pile of corn. One night she crossed a river in a rowboat. It was so dark she could not see the man who rowed the boat.

Many nights she walked alone through the woods and the swamps. On clear nights the North Star was her guide. And when clouds hid the stars, she found her way North by touching the trees. She knew that thick moss grew on the northern side of the trees.

After days and nights of walking and hiding, she reached the state of Pennsylvania. Now she was safe. Nobody would make her go back to Maryland. Pennsylvania was a free state. No one in that state was allowed to own slaves. And most people in Pennsylvania were glad to help runaway slaves.

"I looked at my hands to see if I was the same person, now that I was free," she said later. "There was such a glory over everything. The sun came like gold through the trees and over the fields, and I felt like I was in Heaven."

Then she thought of her family back in Maryland, and she made a promise to herself.

"I had crossed the line of which I had so long been dreaming," she said later. "I was free, but there was no one to welcome me to the land of freedom. I was a stranger in a strange land. And my home, after all, was down with the old folks and my brothers and sisters. But I was free and THEY should be free. I would make a home in the North, and with the Lord helping me, I would bring them all here!"

Remembering your reading

1 What was a "station" on the Underground Railroad?
2 What did a "station master" do?
3 Why did the slaves have to use code words about the Underground Railroad?
4 Why did escaping slaves follow the North Star?
5 What do you think Harriet's brothers were afraid of?
6 Where did Harriet hide?

7 What did she do if it was too cloudy to see the North Star?
8 What did Harriet decide to do after she was free?

Harriet did return South, in disguise, to lead her parents and brothers to safety in the North. She went back many times to guide other slaves to freedom — and was given a code name.

Part 3 Night-time, Daytime

It is now five years before the beginning of the civil war. On the plantations of Maryland when they talk about Harriet, they call her Moses. In the North, too, she is known as Moses.

In the little slave cabins they whisper her name and hope she will come soon. In the big plantation houses, the masters wonder, "Who is this person they call Moses?"

Night-time

A song is sung outside the slave cabins:

Go down, Moses,
Way down to Egypt land
And tell old Pharaoh
To let my people go.

A slave whispers to his wife, "She is here. Get the children ready."

The next morning an overseer counts six slaves missing. Moses again!

Daytime

A Negro woman walks down the street. A big sunbonnet covers her face. She carries two chickens and walks bent over, like an old woman.

Suddenly she sees a white man coming toward her. Quickly she lets go of the chickens. The man laughs to see the old woman chasing two chickens across the road.

As soon as he is out of sight, the woman laughs too. Her trick has worked. The man did not recognise her. The man was her old master. The woman was Moses again!

Night-time

In Wilmington, Delaware, the house of Thomas Garrett is being watched. Everyone knows he is a friend of the slaves. Everyone knows he hides them in his house. He even gives them food and money and shoes. The people who keep watch over his house would like to catch him helping a runaway slave. They would get a reward for returning the slave to his master.

The door of Thomas Garrett's house opens. Here he is! But the woman with him can't be a slave! She walks like a great lady. And her gray silk gown and heavy gray veil are the clothes of a lady. Mr Garrett takes her arm and leads her to the carriage. The carriage drives away — with Moses again!

Daytime

A woman sits in a railroad station. Nearby two men are talking about a big reward.

"Forty thousand dollars for Harriet Tubman, dead or alive," one of the men says.

Then the men see the Negro woman sitting in the station. They stare at the deep scars on her neck. Quickly the woman opens a book and pretends to read it. She hears one of the men say. "That can't be the woman we want. Harriet Tubman can't read or write!"

But it IS Harriet Tubman. It is the one they call Moses!

adapted from *Runaway Slave* by Ann McGovern

Remembering your reading

1 Why does everyone call Harriet "Moses"?
2 Which do you think was the cleverest of her tricks or disguises? Which was her luckiest escape?

63

Harriet Tubman's Character

Making Notes

This word square hides 20 words you could use to describe Harriet Tubman and tell the story of her life. When you find a word, write it down and try to remember something that Harriet did that showed you what sort of person she was.

Make some notes, like this:

Harriet Tubman was a very brave girl, who escaped from slavery alone, and returned after she was free to help other slaves escape. She first showed her bravery when....
She must have been very scared during her journey.
She thought of .....

How many more words can you think of to describe Harriet? Add them to your list, with examples of what she did.

I	B	D	F	A	I	T	H	F	U	L	R	N	E
N	S	C	A	R	E	D	A	E	F	D	H	S	C
D	D	B	R	A	V	E	P	A	R	A	O	W	L
Q	U	I	C	K	Q	U	P	R	E	R	P	R	E
S	T	O	D	L	U	T	Y	F	E	I	E	E	V
T	I	G	E	N	E	R	O	U	S	N	F	L	E
R	R	L	B	L	O	N	E	L	Y	G	U	I	R
O	E	T	H	O	U	G	H	T	F	U	L	E	D
N	D	N	D	I	S	G	U	I	S	E	D	V	S
G	W	E	D	D	E	T	E	R	M	I	N	E	D
U	N	S	E	L	F	I	S	H	L	P	E	D	N
G	R	E	S	O	U	R	C	E	F	U	L	V	S

Your Writing: Description

Write a paragraph describing the kind of person Harriet was.

Planning

Your list of words and examples (your notes) will not be in any sensible order. You probably did not write complete sentences. You may not want to use all your notes — only the more important ones.

Decide which of your notes you will use first. Which ones will you use next? Choose the order carefully.

Rewrite your notes in sentences as you go along. You might rewrite the notes above the word square like this:

Brave - ran away from Miss Susan; went on alone without her brothers; went back to save others.
Scared - when she thought of slave-catchers' dogs.

Revising

When you have finished, read what you have written, to check that it is clear and makes sense. Turn to page 15 if you are not sure what to look for.

Proofreading

Search for any mistakes you have made because you were working quickly.

Ask someone else to read your work and tell you if there is anything they don't understand.

Drama or Writing a Play

Here are three ideas for drama or playwriting. If you are writing a play, turn to page 21 to remind yourself how to set it out.

☆ A group of slaves are talking at night, in secret. They have heard bad news — their master has lost all his money.
  What will happen to them?
  What stories do they tell?
  What are they afraid of?
  What will they do?

☆ An escaping slave arrives at a "station" on the "Underground Railroad".
  What stories has he or she to tell of the dangers of the journey so far?
  What warnings will the "station master" give?
  What will they plan for the next stage?

☆ Harriet helps some slaves to escape under the noses of their masters.
  What tricks do they think up?
  Do they use disguise?
  Do they try to distract the masters' attention?

Harriet Tubman — This Is Your Life
Group Work
You can share the writing or act it out for the rest of the class or other classes.

If you act it out, the speakers will need notes to help them.

The characters will be:

Harriet

The presenter of the show

People who can tell part of Harriet's life story, like

Her parents and brothers

Miss Susan

People who remember Harriet's escape

People who escaped with Harriet's help

People who later found out they'd been tricked by a clever disguise.

What to do
Start by passing round and reading each other's pieces of writing about Harriet.

Each person called to appear in the show will have a story to tell, and say what sort of person Harriet is — so the writing you have done, and your set of notes, will come in useful.

Some characters in the show can use the stories they have read. Some of them will want to make up stories about Harriet. The ideas for drama and playwriting will help you to make up good stories.

Everyone will need a copy of the order in which characters appear, and the stories they tell. Set it out like this:

Scene	Characters Speaking	Story to be told
1.	Presenter: Harriet	Why she is called Moses – Introduction
2.	Presenter: Edward Brodas	How he hired Harriet to Miss Susan
3.	Presenter: Miss Susan	What happened while Harriet worked for her
4.	Presenter: Harriet	How she escaped from Miss Susan's, why she went back.....
5	?　　　　?	?　　　　?

Other things to do

Maps
Copy or trace the map on page 58. Write a sentence about each of the places marked. Say why they were important to Harriet Tubman.

Poems
Read "*I'm Going to Leave You*" (page 60) again to remind yourself of Harriet's journey. Work out a poem about the journey. Here are some starters to help you arrange your ideas.

Choose a word that is important in the story. Write the letters down the page. Use each letter to start a new line of the poem.

FREEDOM

Frightened, I listened for the days
Rest came to me only in hiding when it was daytime.
Every night . . . .
E . . . .
D . . . .
O . . . .
M . . . .

Draw a shape and write the words of your poem to fit the shape.

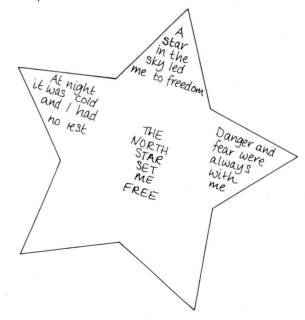

A star in the sky led me to freedom

At night it was cold and I had no rest

THE NORTH STAR SET ME FREE

Danger and fear were always with me

Fears and Superstitions

Contents

Superstitions	Strange Happenings	Mansions of Mystery	Other things to do
Magical Possibilities	Four Short Stories	The Devils of Rose Hall	Magicians
Superstition	Discussion and Storytelling	The Curse of Rose Hall	Magic Potions
Your Writing: Poems	Fears	The Listeners	Magic Words
	Lost at Night	The "Kreepy Castle"	Spells and Charms
	Your Writing: Personal	Your Writing: Stories	

Superstitions

Richard is a black boy, growing up in the southern states of America in the 1930s. His life is very hard. The one way he can make things turn out well for himself is by using his imagination, so in his mind he makes the world a magical place. Here he tells all his superstitions.

Magical Possibilities

Up or down the wet or dusty streets, indoors or out, the days and nights began to spell out magic possibilities.

If I walked under a leaning ladder, I would certainly have bad luck.

If my right ear itched, then something good was being said about me by somebody.

If I placed a safety pin on a steel railroad track and let a train run over it, the safety pin would turn into a pair of bright brand-new scissors.

If it rained while the sun was shining, then the Devil was beating his wife.

If I broke a mirror, I would have seven years of bad luck.

If I had a cold and tied a worn, dirty sock about my throat before I went to bed, the cold would be gone next morning.

If I wore a bit of asafetida* in a little bag tied about my neck, I would never catch a disease.

If a man confessed anything on his deathbed, it was the truth, for no man could stare death in the face and lie.

If I spilt salt, I should toss a pinch over my left shoulder to ward off misfortune.

from *Black Boy* by Richard Wright

asafetida — gum from a tree. It tastes and smells like onion or garlic.

1 Do you believe any of these superstitions, or any like them?

2 Some of them are more like "sayings" which parents might tell their children. Which ones? Have you heard any "sayings" like these? Can you think of more?

3 Do you think there are explanations or reasons for any of these strange superstitions or sayings?

4 Make your own list, or class list, of superstitions and sayings.

Superstition

I know
    that when a grumbling old woman
Is the first thing I meet in the morning
    I must rush back to bed
    And cover my head.
That wandering sheep on a sultry afternoon
Are really men come from their dark graves
    To walk in light
    In mortal sight.
That when my left hand or eyelid twitches
Or when an owl hoots from a nearby tree
    I should need pluck.
    It means bad luck;
That drink spilled goes to ancestral spirits,
That witches dance in clumps of bananas;
That crumbs must be left in pots and plates
    Until the morn
    For babes unborn.
That it's wrong to stand in doorways at dusk
For the ghosts must pass — they have right of way!
That when a hidden root trips me over
    Fault's not in my foot.
    It's an evil root.
That if I sleep with feet towards the door
    I'll not long be fit.
    I know it — Yes I know it!

                  Minji Karibo

1   Read the poem again. Notice, as you do so, how the writer has set out the superstitions as lines of a poem and made some of them rhyme.

2   Make a list, using your own words, of the superstitions in this poem.

3   In the last line, the person telling the poem says, "I know it — Yes I know it!" What do you think this line really means?

Your Writing: Poems

Write your own poem called "Superstition".
Here's one way to do it —

    Choose the most dramatic and striking of the superstitions and sayings that you have come across. For each one, think about the best way to set it out as lines of a poem.

The poem on this page starts off with: "I know". Decide whether to start it off with that.

    Or you could start with: "People say" or "Sometimes I believe" or "I heard".

    Or you could have a different phrase before each different superstition.

    This poem ends with "I know it — Yes I know it." You could end your poem with your thoughts about what you really think about the superstitions.

Strange Happenings

The four stories below were told or written by children. Read them over and discuss each one.

The Dream

I had this dog and it was ill, and some people killed it and I never knew about it. My mum never told me. One night I had a dream about how it was dead; all ants trampled over it and people were stepping on it, and all the bones were scattered all over the street. Then when I got up next morning my mum told me it was dead, and then when I went downstairs that evening I was looking about and then I saw my dog. It came all red and then it went away. Then when I went upstairs and told my mum my dog's downstairs, and she said, "Oh no, it ain't, it's dead, it died a long time ago."

Yvonne

1 In this story, the dog, who is really dead, appears twice to Yvonne. What does the dog look like? When does it appear?
2 Why do you think the dog appeared to her? Why did it look as it did?
3 Why do you think her mum hadn't told her about the death of her dog?

The Chain

This woman, she lives by the church. Every morning, every Sunday morning she goes to church and gets Holy Communion. And she was a witch as well because my dad said one night he came from a club, and he felt a chain on his foot, but he couldn't see the chain and it kept on ringing in his foot. He kept on falling over but he couldn't see the chain, and so when he was by the mountain then he saw the person and it was this lady. . . . She was a witch and so she kept on pulling the chain and my dad couldn't see the chain and every morning she goes for Holy Communion but after a while and my dad saw her my dad said hallo she wouldn't even answer.

She was a witch, she wears black clothes, she goes out in the night-time, dark in the night-time.

Ann-Marie

1 Why did Ann-Marie think the woman was a witch? Do you think that she could have been a witch?
2 Why do you think Ann-Marie's father told her this story?

The Black and White Hands

Once when I was in the West Indies, I heard a story about the black and white hands. Once this lady, and her husband went to England to have a holiday, and these black and white hands kept knocking on her door, from three o'clock in the morning till six o'clock at night. The black and white hand was knocking at the door. The lady had two children. She told the children to open the door. Meanwhile she looked through the window. The children opened the door, then the black and white hands came through and strangled her little children. Then the black and white hands went to the next flat. It was underneath where the black and white hands started to strangle people, and it strangled the two babies of a lady. Then when the lady came back from her shopping, she saw her two babies strangled. Then she phoned up the police, and the police said she must put a cross on her door, and a red cross on her pillow and a red chair in the room.

Sandra

1 What things did the police tell the lady she must do? Why?
2 Do you think this story could be true? If not, where do you think Sandra got her ideas from?

The Tunnel Disaster

Mr Briggs was driving a train from London to Edinburgh non-stop when he noticed some figures on the line, just in front of the tunnel. He pulled on the brakes and the train ground to a halt. He looked up and the figures had vanished. He went to see a doctor who told him that he was seeing things.

About one year later the day started normally for Mr. Briggs. He took his train from Euston station up to Edinburgh. After having a brief snack, he started back from Edinburgh to London. As he came to that same tunnel he saw some figures on the line, five of them to be exact. His hand hesitated on the brake and he rubbed his eyes. By then it was too late. The scream of dying men and the sound of flesh against metal filled the tunnel. The realisation suddenly dawned on him; he had cut down five linesmen.

In court it was decided that he should spend five days in a mental hospital and if their report was good he should be released.

Mr Briggs is now an old man but he remembers clearly the night of the tunnel disaster.

Mark

1   Was the doctor right to tell Mr Briggs that "he was seeing things"?
2   Does the story tell you whose fault it was that the five linesmen died?
3   Have you ever been told that "you must be seeing things"? Have you ever said that to anyone else?

Discussion and Storytelling

☆ Do you believe these four stories? Has anything like them ever happened to you? Have you ever heard other stories like them?

☆ Decide what is the strangest happening that you know of.

☆ Tell each other these happenings and discuss them:

Do you believe them and take them seriously?
Do you treat them as a joke?
Do you believe in ghosts and spirits?
Why do some people believe in them?
Can you think of any good ghost stories?
Why are ghost stories enjoyable?
Why do people enjoy being frightened?

Telling Stories and Writing Stories

1   Which of the four stories do you think were told aloud, and which were written?
2   What are the differences between them which

show which were told and which were written?

3   Note down any words or expressions, or other differences which show whether the story was told or written. Set it out like this:

	Spoken Stories	Written Stories
Words		
Expressions		
Other Differences		

Fears

When are the times we feel frightened and afraid?
Sometimes it's on very ordinary occasions:

I'm alone in the evening
when the family sits
reading and sleeping
and I watch the fire in close
to see flame goblins
wriggling out of their caves
for the evening

Later I'm alone
when the bath has gone cold around me
and I have put my foot
beneath the cold tap
where it can dribble
through the valley between my toes
out across the white plain of my foot
and bibble bibble into the sea

I'm alone
when mum's switched out the light
my head against the pillow
listening to ca thump ca thump
in the middle of my ears.
It's my heart.

Michael Rosen

Lost at Night

In this piece the writer is trying to get across what it was like for one boy on one occasion when he was frightened.

Swami, an Indian boy, has run away from home because his father has been angry with him because he was doing badly at school. Swami is afraid that his father will stop him from playing in a cricket match that he has been looking forward to, so he decides to hide away for a few days and then come back for the match. He walks out of his town and then . . .

Night fell suddenly, and his heart beat fast. His throat went dry as he realised that he had not reached the main road. The trees were still thick and the road was still narrow. The main road was broader, and there the sky was not screened through branches. But here one could hardly see the sky; the stars gleamed through occasional gaps overhead. He quickened his pace though he was tired. He ran a little distance, his feet falling on the leaf-covered ground with a sharp rustling noise.

The birds in the branches overhead started at this noise and fluttered their wings. In that deep darkness and stillness the noise of the fluttering wings had an uncanny ghostly quality. Swami was frightened and stood still. He must reach the main road and find his way home. He would not mind even if it were twelve o'clock when he reached the road. Here the closeness of the tree-trunks and their branches intertwining at the top gave the road the appearance of a black, bleak cavern with an evil spirit brooding over it.

He started on again. He trod warily so as not to make a noise and disturb the birds again, though he felt an urge to run, run with all his might and reach the main road and home. The conflict between the impulse to run and the caution that counselled him not to run was fierce. As he walked noiselessly, slowly, suppressing the impulse to run on madly, his nerves quivered with the strain. It was as if he had been rope-walking in a gale.

His ears heard every noise. They caught every noise his feet made. His feet came down on the ground with a light tick or a subdued crackle or a gentle swish, according to what was on the ground: small dry twigs, half-green leaves, or a thick layer of dry withered leaves. There were occasional patches of bare uncovered ground, and there the noise was a light thud, or pit-pat; pit-pat-pit-pat in monotonous repetition. His feet said pish-pish-pat-pit-swish and crackled. These noises streamed into his head, monotonously, endlessly. They were like sinister whispers, calling him to a dreadful sacrifice. He clearly heard his name whispered. There was no doubt about it. "Swami . . . Swami . . . Swami . . . Swami . . . Swami" the voice said, and then the dreadful suggestion of a sacrifice. It was some devil, coming behind him noiselessly, and saying the same thing over and over again, deep into his ears. He stopped and looked about. There the immense monster crouched, with its immense black legs wide apart, and its shadowy arms joined over its head. It swayed a little. He dared not take his eyes off it for fear that it might pounce upon him. He stood frozen to the ground and stared at this monster.

Why did it cease its horrid whispers the moment he turned back? He stood staring. He might have spent about five minutes thus. And when the first thrill of fear subsided, he saw a little more clearly and found that the monster consisted of massive tree trunks and their top branches.

from Swami and Friends by R. K. Narayan

Do you think the writer has made the boy's fear seem real?

Answer these questions to help you decide.

1 What was this monster, really?
2 Why did it stop whispering the moment he turned back to look at it?
3 Why is Swami seeing and hearing monsters?
4 Why is it very dark on that road?
5 What was the first noise which had frightened Swami?
6 Why did he feel "as if he had been rope-walking in a gale"?
7 Why are his ears so sharp and sensitive, hearing every little noise?

Your Writing: Personal

☆ **A Time I was Frightened**

or

☆ **The Strangest Happening**

Planning

Remember the strange happenings you discussed after the last section. Think about times you have been frightened. Tell them to each other. Do you agree that when you are frightened, all your senses, your hearing, sight, smell, taste and touch all become very sharp and sensitive? Can you think of times when this was true? Decide which experience will make a good piece of writing.

Drafting

Try it out. Aim to make the reader feel the fear you experienced or the weirdness of the happening. Include details of what was seen, heard, smelt and so on at the most important moment of the story.

Revising

Ask someone to read your writing. Ask them whether you have made the experience real to the reader. (Use the questions on page 15 to help).

Mansions of Mystery

Many stories which are frightening or mysterious have a scary place or building as a big feature. Can you think of any stories like this? Is there a place you know which everybody thinks is haunted or where nobody dares to go?

Read these pieces on this topic.

The Devils of Rose Hall

You don't have to believe this story. My uncle told it to me long ago; but my uncle didn't always tell the truth, so make up your own mind.

In 1920, Rose Hall Great House (the famous haunted Great House overlooking the blue Caribbean sea on the north coast of Jamaica) lay in ruins. No one had lived in the house for over fifty years. There it stood alone on the hills rising from the green cane fields. No other houses were ever built close to it. The manager's house and the labourers' cottages were as far away as possible, down near the beach, almost out of sight.

My uncle was a young fellow in those days, and he knew all the other young fellows hanging out around Falmouth and Montego Bay. They went bird-shooting and swimming together. But no one would stay long near that empty ruin.

The country people all around said that the devil lived there, and anyone who slept in the house would die violently and mysteriously during the night, or survive hopelessly insane.

But people did go into the house from time to time. My uncle did, for one, with some of his friends. They visited it in broad daylight, of course, and walked through the grand rooms thick with dust, down the narrow back stairs to the cellars where the infamous Annie Palmer used to practise black magic, and past the dark brown stain on the wall which, they say, is the blood of her last murdered husband.

No, Rose Hall wasn't a nice place at all, even in bright sunshine.

The windows were broken for the most part, and otherwise black with dust and grime. Cobwebs were everywhere, and hundreds of spiders of all sizes and colours were having a wonderful time raising large families and working industriously to bring them up. Rats lived there too: the kind of big, brown rats that stare at you like a prosecuting attorney, rats which wear seven-league boots and go down the wooden stairs "clump — clump — CLUMP — *slither* — CRASSSSSH!" There were tribes and generations of these rats. And then there were mice, which chewed and chewed and chewed at goodness knows what behind the mahogany panelling in the bedrooms and dressing rooms, and carried on sudden conversations in high squeaks and whispers.

One thing you could be sure of: Rose Hall was not really *empty*, what with the rats and mice and spiders. And it was never really quiet either.

It sounded very still when you pushed open the creaking front door and stood in the weather-beaten hall. But soon you would hear furtive whispers, tiny footfalls, and the echo of noises which you had not made.

from *The Devils of Rose Hall* by Jean De Costa

1 Find two reasons why the country people did not go near Rose Hall at night.
2 What does the writer tell you about Rose Hall that makes it sound a spooky place?
3 Make a list of all the words, phrases and details in the story that create a mysterious atmosphere.

Rose Hall was the home of Annie Palmer, known as the White Witch, because so many who lived with her mysteriously disappeared.

This poem imagines what happens after her death.

The Curse of Rose Hall

Darkness hangs thick on the haunted air
And a ghostly jury in session there
Lays Annie Palmer's foul deeds bare
In the ruined rooms of Rose Hall.

Oh white in the daylight the stone walls gleam
And gracious and spacious the vast rooms seem
And the poison and murderings all a dream,
And the frightened ghosts of Rose Hall.

But on moonless evenings when Patoo calls
And no clear brightness from heaven falls
Then into the ruins of splendid halls
Slink the vengeful ghosts of Rose Hall.

Up from its cellars and nameless graves
Slouch husband, and lovers, and strong black
    slaves.
And she looks in vain for the face that saves.
But each wants revenge for Rose Hall.

The deadly evidence tolls its bell
As one by one the victims tell
Of how they lived in that witch's hell
With the wicked Queen of Rose Hall.

Proud Annie hears what they tell about
And she savagely tries to curse them out,
But nobody there can hear her shout.
For all are dead at Rose Hall.

With fury she listens to their tale
And not for repentance does she pale —
But to know that her obeah* could fail,
And bring her death at Rose Hall.

When the last of the shuddering victims spoke
The jury its ghostly silence broke,
And bound the White Witch with a fearful yoke
To the ruined stones of Rose Hall.

Now on secret nights when the sky is blind
And Patoo* mocks what his sharp eyes find
You can hear Annie's bitter sobs behind
The crumbling walls of Rose Hall.

Alma Norman

obeah — witchcraft
Patoo — the Owl

1 What is the "ghostly jury" doing?
2 When do the "vengeful ghosts" appear?
3 Why do the ghosts appear?
4 Why does "proud Annie" grow pale as she listens to what the ghosts tell?
5 What is the verdict of the jury?
6 What is the punishment Annie has to suffer?
7 How does each verse end? How does each verse rhyme? What tone of voice do you think it's best to read the poem in?
8 Make a list of all the words, phrases and details in the poem that create a mysterious atmosphere.

The Listeners

"Is there anybody there?" said the Traveller,
Knocking on the moonlit door;
And his horse in the silence champed the grasses
Of the forest's ferny floor:
And a bird flew up out of the turret,
Above the Traveller's head:
And he smote upon the door again a second time;
"Is there anybody there?" he said.

But no-one descended to the Traveller;
No head from the leaf-fringed sill
Leaned over and looked into his grey eyes,
Where he stood perplexed and still.
But only a host of phantom listeners
That dwelt in the lone house then
Stood listening in the quiet of the moonlight
To that voice from the world of men:
Stood thronging the faint moonbeams on the dark
        stair,
That goes down to the empty hall,
Hearkening in an air stirred and shaken
By the lonely Traveller's call.
And he felt in his heart their strangeness
Their stillness answering his cry
While his horse moved, cropping the dark turf,
'Neath the starred and leafy sky;
For he suddenly smote on the door, even
Louder, and lifted his head:—
"Tell them I came, and no-one answered,
That I kept my word," he said.

Never the least stir made the listeners,
Though every word he spake
Fell echoing through the shadowiness of the still
        house
From the one man left awake:
Ay, they heard his foot upon the stirrup,
And the sound of iron on stone,
And how the silence surged softly backward,
When the plunging hoofs were gone.

Walter de la Mare

1   Who are the Listeners?
2   Who is the Traveller?
3   What is the place?
4   What details has the writer put in to create a sense
    of mystery?
5   Make a list of all the words, phrases and details in
    the poem that create a mysterious atmosphere.

74

The Kreepy Kastle

Dinah-Mo and the Dinah Mob are being challenged to spend half-an-hour in "The Kreepy Kastle".

1 What ghostly things might Dinah-Mo see and hear in and around the "Kreepy Kastle"? Make a list.
2 Make a list of words which describe what all these ghostly things might do in the Kreepy Kastle (like howl, creak) and a list of what Dinah-Mo and her friends might do (like tremble, shiver).
3 Make lists of words which describe the Kastle, and the things in it (musty, cold, eerie); and words which describe how Dinah-Mo and her friends feel (startled, petrified, cold, clammy).
4 Tell a story of Dinah-Mo, in the Kreepy Kastle. Make it *as short as possible* BUT try to use as many of the words on your lists as you can.

Your Writing: Stories

Choose one of these stories to write.

☆ **A Mansion of Mystery**
Create a place which is mysterious, frightening and awesome. Tell the story of someone who came to learn its secrets.

☆ **The Devils of Rose Hall**
Someone is brave enough to spend the night in Rose Hall. Write a chilling tale of how he or she was persuaded to do this and what happened during the night and the next day.

☆ **Dinah-Mo in the Kreepy Kastle**
Rewrite your Dinah-Mo story, but make it much longer. Show how Dinah-Mo stands up to all the spooky happenings. What is the true reason for all the ghastly goings-on? What does she do about it?

As you plan, draft and revise your story, have the lists of words you made in front of you. Can you use any of them to improve your story?

Sort out these words into those you could use to describe **ghostly sights**, **ghostly sounds**, and **people's feelings**.

ghostly	awesome	looming
eerie	ominous	weird
awed	musty	damp
macabre	shivering	diabolical
rustling	quavering	ghoulish
trembling	horrible	paralysed
shadowy	moaning	swirling
crashing	spectral	uncanny

Other things to do

Make a collection of pieces of writing and illustrations on the theme of:

MAGIC, MAGICIANS AND THE MYSTERIOUS

Look at the words in the lists you made for the "Kreepy Kastle". Turn some of these words into pictures, like these:

Magicians   Write a description, a poem or a story about a magician and draw a picture.

Magic Potions   Make up a recipe for a "magic potion" that the magician uses to make the magic work.

Say the Magic Words   Make a collection of old and new "magic words" and chants.

Spells and Charms   Make up good and bad spells!

In the following pages, you'll find things to read which will help you with most of these tasks.

You may be able to find some poems and drawings in books to add to your collection. Keep an eye out in the newspapers for reports of new strange happenings.

When you have finished, make a tape-recording of the pieces of writing you enjoy most.

Magicians

Think of all the characters in stories you know who do magic. What do they look like?

What does a witch look like? Is your picture of a witch — an old woman with a black cloak and a tall pointed hat who flies through the air on a broom-stick? Here's a story by an eleven year old girl in which she uses this idea of a witch to frighten a friend:

A Ghost Story

When we were small we lived in a cottage in Pound Lane at number five. In number seven was an old man called Sid. He had a hump on his back. At number three was a lady in black with a black dog and a black cat. We called her Winney the Witch.

One day a friend of ours came to stay for a week. It was winter time, very cold and very windy. We were sitting by the fire telling each other about different things.

We told her that Winny came round some nights and would tap on the window and call her husband and that Old Sid came round as well looking for cats' bodies in the garden.

By then it was time to go to bed. She did not want to go but we told her that the story wasn't true. But when she was in bed we let a button down on a piece of string to tap on the window. We left the door at the back open as it always made a squeaky noise and she was really frightened.

We did it once more and she came running up to us because it frightened her so. At that moment we looked out of the window and we stood there still as Sid was out the back with a light. We all could not stop yelling. By this time Mum and Dad were awake. We all got a telling off and were told to get back into bed but all night long every little noise and scrape and squeak made us shake.

It was bad and any time the wind blew the house would shake and that made it worse. My friend did not stay any longer and we found out the next morning that Old Sid was looking for the cat, but not a dead one, it was his pet one. We did not tell any more stories.

This is a true story my mum told, about when she was a very little girl.

Tracey

The Griesly Wife

"Lie still, my newly married wife,
    Lie easy as you can.
You're young and ill-accustomed yet
    To sleeping with a man."

The snow lay thick, the moon was full
    And shone across the floor
The young wife went with never a word
    Barefooted to the door.

He up and followed sure and fast,
    The moon shone clear and white.
But before his coat was on his back
    His wife was out of sight.

He trod the trail wherever it turned
    By many a mound and scree,
And still the barefoot track led on
    And an angry man was he.

He followed fast, he followed slow,
    And still he called her name,
But only the dingoes of the hills
    Yowled back at him again.

His hair stood up along his neck,
    His angry mind was gone,
For the track of the two bare feet gave out
    And a four-foot track went on.

Her nightgown lay upon the snow
    As it might upon the sheet,
But the track that led on from where it lay
    Was never of human feet.

His heart turned over in his chest,
    He looked from side to side
And he thought more of his gumwood fire
    Than he did of his griesly bride.

And first he started walking back
    And then he began to run
And his quarry wheeled at the end of her track
    And hunted him in turn.

Oh, long the fire may burn for him
    And open stand the door,
And long the bed may wait empty:
    He'll not be back any more.

John Manifold

1 Explain what you think happened to the "griesly wife".
2 What do you think the creature whose track "was never of human feet" looks like?
3 How do you explain the mysterious happenings in the story?
4 Why is the poem called "The Griesly Wife"?

Magic Potions

When people thought of witches casting their spells, they imagined them brewing a horrid potion in a cauldron over a fire to make their magic work. This is what Shakespeare thought might go in the brew:

The Witches' Brew

First Witch	Round about the cauldron go;
	In the poisoned entrails throw.
	Toad, that under cold stone
	Days and nights has thirty-one
	Sweltered venom, sleeping got,
	Boil thou first i' the charmed pot.
All	Double, double, toil and trouble;
	Fire burn and cauldron bubble.
Second Witch	Fillet of a fenny snake,
	In the cauldron boil and bake;
	Eye of newt, and toe of frog,
	Wool of bat and tongue of dog,
	Adder's fork and blindworm's
	sting,
	Lizard's leg and howlet's wing,
	For a charm of powerful trouble,
	Like a hell-broth boil and bubble.
All	Double, double, toil and trouble;
	Fire burn and cauldron bubble.
Second Witch	Cool it with a baboon's blood,
	Then the charm is firm and good.

Write out this recipe, or one of your own, and illustrate it.

Magic Words

People still have the idea of "saying the magic words" to make things happen. People, especially children, still sing or chant rhymes for many different reasons:

to make fun of somebody:
Mrs White had a fright
In the middle of the night
She saw a ghost eating toast
Halfway up a lamp post.

for skipping or hand-clapping:
I saw Esau sawing wood
And Esau saw I saw him,
Though Esau saw I saw him saw
Still Esau went on sawing

As I sat under the apple tree
A birdie sent his love to me,
And as I wiped it from my eye,
I said, Thank goodness, cows can't fly.

or just for a joke:
One fine day in the middle of the night,
Two dead men got up to fight,
Back to back they faced each other,
Drew their swords and shot each other.
A paralysed donkey passing by
Kicked a blind man in the eye,
Knocked him through a nine inch wall
Into a dry ditch and drowned them all.

to start a game:
Innerty fenerty fickety fage,
El dell dominage,
Urky blurkey starry rock
Black pudden white trout
That shows you're out.

Think about times when people say or sing things together. Think about what they chant and what the purpose of the chant is. Can you think of at least one chant, and its purpose for each of the following places? The playground, in school, a place of worship, a sporting gathering, a family celebration?

People in other societies and countries use chants too.

This chant for killing a snake comes from Cuba.

Sensemaya: A Chant for Killing a Snake

Mayombe-bombe-mayombe!
Mayombe-bombe-mayombe!
Mayombe-bombe-mayombe!

The snake has eyes of glass;
the snake comes and coils itself round a pole;
with his eyes of glass, round a pole,
with his eyes of glass.
The snake walks without legs;
the snake hides in the grass;
walking he hides in the grass
walking without legs.

Mayombe-bombe-mayombe!
Mayombe-bombe-mayombe!
Mayombe-bombe-mayombe!

If you hit him with an axe he will die.
Hit him hard!
Do not hit him with your foot, he will bite,
do not hit him with your foot, he is going away!

Sensemaya, the snake,
Sensemaya.
Sensemaya, with his eyes,
Sensemaya.
Sensemaya, with his tongue,
Sensemaya.
Sensemaya, with his mouth,
Sensemaya —

Dead snake cannot eat;
dead snake cannot hiss;
cannot walk,
cannot run.
Dead snake cannot look;
dead snake cannot drink;
cannot breathe,
cannot bite.

Mayombe-bombe-mayombe!
Sensemaya, the snake —
Mayombe-bombe-mayombe!
Sensemaya, it is still —
Mayombe-bombe-mayombe!
Sensemaya, the snake —
Mayombe-bombe-mayombe!
Sensemaya, it is dead.

Nicholas Guillen

Spells and Charms

People might go to witches or magicians if they wanted them to cast a spell, good or bad, to make something happen.

Here's a dreadful spell from North American Indians:

A Spell to Destroy Life

Listen!
Now I have come to step over your soul
(I know your clan)
(I know your name)
(I have stolen your spirit and buried it under
the earth)
I bury your soul under the earth
I cover you over with black rock
I cover you over with black cloth
I cover you over with black slabs
You disappear forever

Your path leads to the
Black Coffin
in the hills of the Darkening Land

This writer has written his own verse to find his lost season ticket!

To Find a Lost Season Ticket

Stay, if fallen on the floor;
Flap, if hidden behind a door;
Jump, if in some guilty pocket;
Hear me, hear me,
Season ticket!
If I sing the spell in vain,
I cannot come to school again.

Ian Serraillier

79

The Canterbury Tales

Contents

The Pilgrimage
  Chaucer's Pilgrims
  Analysing Characters

A Modern Journey
  A Church Excursion
  Some Characters
  Your Writing: Description

The Story Competition
  The Pardoner's Tale
  Storytelling or Drama
  The Nun's Priest's Tale
  A Story with a Moral

Other things to do
  Chaucer's English
  The Miller
  Decorated Letters

The Pilgrimage to Canterbury

Whan that Aprill with his shoures soote
The droghte of March hath perced to the roote . . .
Thanne longen folke to goon on pilgrimages,
And specially from every shires ende
Of Engelond to Caunterbury they wende,
The holy blisful martir for to seke,
That hem hath holpen whan that they were seeke.

When the sweet showers of April
pierce the dryness of March . . .
Then the people long to go on pilgrimages
And especially from every county of England
They go to Canterbury
To see the holy blissful martyr
Who gives them help when they are sick.

This is the beginning of one of the most famous pieces of writing in English, Geoffrey Chaucer's "Canterbury Tales". It was written about 1380, at a time when the Church was very powerful, and a sign of living a good religious life was to go on a pilgrimage. In England, people would often journey to Canterbury, where Thomas Becket, the "holy blissful martyr" had been murdered.

Thomas was made Archbishop of Canterbury by King Henry II, two hundred years before Chaucer wrote his Tales. The King hoped that Thomas would help him gain power over the Church. But Thomas was very religious and defended the freedom of the Church against Henry's efforts to control it. When four of Henry's knights murdered Thomas in Canterbury cathedral, the ordinary people were shocked. People reported having visions and dreams about Thomas, and stories grew up that he could cure the sick.

So Canterbury became a centre of pilgrimage, where people could see the scene of the murder, visit Thomas's shrine, and pray for his help in their lives.

1 Pick out all the reasons why people came to think of Thomas as a saint. Decide whether you think they are good reasons.
2 Can you think of any modern examples of people who have become very famous after their death? Are all these people religious?
3 Think of as many places of pilgrimage as you can and the famous people associated with those places.
4 Why do people go on pilgrimages?

Chaucer's Pilgrims

Geoffrey Chaucer goes on:

"... Well it so happened that one day at that time of year I was at the Tabard Inn in Southwark ready to go on a pilgrimage to Canterbury when into the inn came a band of twenty-nine people of all different sorts, who all meant to ride on a pilgrimage to Canterbury.

Before I go on, let me tell you about some members of this merry company ...

The Nun

There were very many people of the Church there, and one of them was a Nun, or Priestess, who smiled very simply and coyly at everyone. She certainly never swore, but sang very sweetly and correctly at services, and spoke French with an English accent, for she certainly had never been to a place like Paris. She had very good table manners at the table, and would never let a morsel of food fall from her lips, but would carry the morsel up to her mouth without letting the smallest drop fall on her breast. Then she would wipe her upper lip so clean that not a trace of grease was to be seen upon the cup after she had drunk. She certainly was very entertaining, agreeable and friendly.

She had ever such tender feelings and would weep piteously if she saw a dead or bleeding mouse caught in a trap. She kept little dogs whom she fed on roasted meat, with fine white bread, and if someone took a stick to one of them and beat them until they hurt, then she would cry bitterly. She was all sentiment and tender heart.

She had an elegant nose, glass-grey eyes, and a very soft, small red mouth, and a fine broad forehead. She wore a brooch on which was engraved: "Love conquers all".

The Monk

There was also a Monk whose great sport was hunting. The jangling of his bridle as he rode about the countryside was as loud as the ringing of the chapel bell. He kept greyhounds to course after hares, and plenty of horses. He wore fine grey fur at his sleeves and an elaborate gold pin to fasten his hood under his chin. His bald patch shone like a mirror and so did his greasy face. His grey eyeballs never seemed to stay in the same place, they glittered like flames beneath a kettle. This was not a pale and tormented priest, but a fat and contented monk.

The Merchant

There was a Merchant with a forked beard who had plenty to say but unfortunately it was his own opinions on the things that he did. He talked so cleverly about his trade that no-one knew that he was really in debt, but all the same he was an excellent fellow although I don't know his name.

The Woman from Bath

From near Bath there came a worthy woman who was some-what deaf, which was a pity. She thought a great deal of herself, and got very cross if in church any lady went before her to the altar steps. She was very interested in clothes — I'm sure that the hat she wore on Sunday weighed ten pounds. She was as I say, a worthy woman and had had five husbands. She had been on many pilgrimages to Rome, France and Germany. She had wide gaps between her teeth. For this occasion she had on a hat as broad as a shield and she wore a flowing cloak that hid her fat hips. She was a jolly lady, laughing and chatting in company.

The Summoner

There was a Summoner* with us in the inn whose face was fiery red because it was covered with horrible pimples. He had narrow eyes, black scabby brows and a thin beard. He had tried all the ointments and creams but nothing could clean up the knobbly white spots sitting on his cheeks. Children ran away when he walked down the street. He loved eating garlic, and onions, and leeks, and drinking red wine until he was fuddled in the head and then he would shout and jabber as if he were crazy and would speak only in Latin."

*The Summoner was a man who summoned people to special Church courts if they had committed an offence against the Church.

Analysing Characters

Chaucer tells us about the pilgrims' appearances and how they behaved. But we can work out quite a lot about their characters from this information.

The Merchant

What does Chaucer tell us about the Merchant?

> Has a forked beard.
>
> Talks a lot, always about himself.
>
> Talks about his trade, but no-one knows he is in debt.
>
> Excellent fellow, but no-one knows. his name.

What do these details tell us about the Merchant's character?

1 Why doesn't the Merchant reveal his name?
2 Why does he cover up the fact he is in debt?
3 Why does he talk so much about himself and his trade?
4 Can he be trusted?
5 Does the forked beard suggest anything?

Make a chart like this for the Monk, the Woman from Bath and the Summoner.

Details Chaucer tells us	What we can work out about the character.	Whether the person is a good person or not.
Forked beard	Sign of someone untrustworthy.	He is not a successful merchant, he is only interested in himself and he is not to be trusted.
Talked a lot about himself	Only thinks of himself.	
Talked about trade. No-one knows he's in debt.	A deceiver and a bankrupt.	
Excellent, fellow but don't know his name.	Doesn't want anyone to know who he is in case he is found out.	

A Modern Journey

A Church Excursion

There were many people going on this trip. There was the vicar, a tall man with a handlebar moustache. He had a small bald patch on the top of his head. He looked rather elegant in his long black garment with a small white dog collar around his neck. He spoke rather posh with a Welsh accent and a lisp. The personality of the vicar was to be a quiet soul — his motto was — live and let die.

There was also a young boy on the trip, a cheeky young tyke. He looked like a bag of laundry. He had small spiked hair. When he laughed a dimple would go in each cheek. He spoke cockney slang. He gets to be all right when you get to know him. He only came for a bit of trouble. He brought his racer with him. He knew he couldn't put it on the coach so we had to wait for him. No one liked him at all.

Now I talk about a lady called Mrs Bromley, a rather plump lady with messy hair. She was always quite noisy. She had a wart on the end of her nose. There isn't much to say about this lady.

There is a person called Mr. Jones. He's always bossing people around. I don't like him. He dresses in a black pin-striped suit. He speaks like a door-to-door salesman.

There has to be one weirdo in the group and I've come to him. He was a hippy. He wore flares and had long hair and was always on about the nuclear war.

Finally there's me, never combing my hair. I wear jeans and a yellow jumper. I talk with a cockney accent. I'm a bit podgey.

Keith

84

A Housewife

The people who were going on the village outing were, first, a housewife who was wearing trousers and a coat. She was middle aged. She was not as kind as she looked but she was not fit or healthy. People said she was a good cook, but I have never eaten her cooking.

Naeem

Tony and Dean

At the back of the line was Tony. He was a tall thin Jamaican with a big Afro. He had a huge stereo on his shoulder and he called it the M.C. Master Blaster. On a leash he had a cat called Mover that had one patch on one eye. Tony was very reluctant to put down his stereo but he eventually did when we got on the coach.

There was a tall guy named Dean and he was a poser. He wore a Gabicci shirt, a lemon Pringle and he had a diamond Pringle around his waist. He had Lois stone-washed jeans, a Fila jacket and Puma Vila's tennis shoes. He was always wanting a fight and I was tempted to give him one but I didn't bother. . . .

Trevor

A Teacher

There was Mr Turner who was a school teacher. He was six foot four and dressed very neatly. He had a short beard that went well with the moustache. He wore reactor light glasses which covered his dark blue eyes. He was often quiet and used to let you play about in class. The children said he was a coffee addict because he often drank coffee. He even had a coffee maker in his room. That is one thing he never let them touch. He wore a brown suit with a nice dotted tie. He was a bachelor. He had ash blond hair. He was not a talker. He often waved but never said hello. He was English. He didn't talk, he just gave out sheets and sat in his chair with a cup of coffee. The children thought he was trying to tease them.

Rodney

Your Writing: Description

1 Decide on a journey that a group of people from all walks of life might go on today: a works' outing? a school trip? a church excursion? a village outing? supporters travelling to their team's away match?

2 Write short descriptions of the people who go on the trip. Tell your readers what the people look like, and how they behave — but try to put over something of their characters by choosing the details carefully, so that the readers can work out what these people are *really* like.

The Story Competition

The innkeeper at the Tabard had a good idea for keeping the pilgrims entertained on their journey. He suggested that they had a storytelling competition: "and the person who tells the best story of all shall be given a free supper here at the Tabard paid for by the rest of us," he said. "I shall come along to be judge and referee and those who don't obey the rules shall pay for what we spend along the way."

A *Pardoner* was an official of the Church who sold people pardons for their sins.

The Pardoner's Tale

My story is of three drunkards who, long before the morning service bell, were sitting in an inn having a drink. As they sat there, they heard the handbell being rung as a coffin was taken down the street to its grave. One of the drunkards called to a boy who worked in the inn:

"Come here, boy. Now run and find out whose body it is they are carrying to the grave. Go on, be quick about it, and make sure you get the name right."

"Please, sir," replied the boy, "there's no need to go. I was told the name two hours before you came here. The man was a friend of yours, and last night he was here in the inn, lying on a bench dead-drunk. That man, that thief, name of Death went up to him and speared him through the heart so that he never even stirred. Please, sir, that Death has killed one thousand people in a plague. You'd better be on the lookout for him sir. My mum says I've got to keep my eyes open for him and not speak to him."

The innkeeper joined in and said, "The boy's right sir. There's a village not a mile from here, and a large village at that, where he has killed every man, woman and child. He's killed so many people around here that I reckon he must live near here."

One of the drunkards got irritated with all this talk and said, "This Death cannot possibly be so very fierce. By God, I am going to search every street for him. Hey mates, look here, the three of us, let's stick together and find and kill this traitor Death who has done away with our friend."

So the three men swore to live and die together and in their drunken rage started off towards the village which the boy and publican had spoken of.

They had gone only about half a mile when they met a very poor old man who greeted them very politely and gently.

"Good morning gentlemen. God be with you."

The loudest-mouthed of the drunkards answered him, "You silly old fool, get out of the way. Why are you so old; isn't it about time you were dead!"

The old man replied, "Sir, I am so old because no-one I have met on my travels, and I have been as far as India, would swop his youth for my age. Not even Death will take my life! So I wander the earth asking, 'When will these bones be laid to rest?' See how I wither, look at my flesh and blood and skin! But you were wrong to speak so roughly to me just now, for one day you will be old and will not like the young to speak to you so. Now if you will excuse me sirs, I shall be on my way."

"Hold your horses old man," said the drunkard, "you don't get off so lightly. I heard you mention a certain traitor, name of Death, who kills all the young men around here. I think you are his spy, and unless you tell us where he is hiding, I'll . . . I'll . . . Well, it'll be the worse for you."

"Ah, now, sirs," the old man said, "if you want to meet Death, turn up the crooked path towards that wood and you'll find him waiting. For all you say, he's not one to hide. You'll find him near that oak-tree — see? May God protect you, and forgive you!"

As soon as the three men heard this, they rushed off but all they found when they reached the tree was a pile of golden florins on the ground. They were all so thrilled at this sight that they completely forgot the real reason for their being there. The wickedest of them said, "Brothers, it is obvious that Fortune has given us this treasure so that we can live in luxury and pleasure. Come let's spend it as we want to.

"Our only problem is how to get the gold away from here. If we walk back into town in broad daylight, people will think we are a gang of robbers and hang us by the neck. No, we must take the treasure back at night and keep it out of sight. I suggest that we draw lots, and he who draws the longest straw shall run back to the town to fetch us bread and wine to last us through the day. Then when night comes we'll all three carry it away as we have planned."

So they drew lots and it fell upon the youngest, and so he set off at once towards the town.

As soon as they had gone, the wicked man sat down and said to the other, "Now friend, look at things this way. You know our mate has gone to get supplies for us, and there lies a pile of gold to be divided equally among three. Now if I could manage it, wouldn't it be better if it was only divided among two?"

"But how could that be?" asked the other. "He knows the gold is here. What could we tell him? What are we to do?"

"First say whether it is a bargain," said the other, "and I will tell you what we shall do."

"Trust me," the second said, "have no fear of that."

"Well," said the wicked man, "we are two, and twice as powerful as he. When he comes back, get up and pretend to wrestle with him in fun, and as you attack, I will stick my dagger in his back and then you draw yours and do the same. Then we can share the money, just between the two of us."

So they agreed to kill the third and youngest of their party.

The youngest, on his way to the town kept thinking about how much better it would be if *he* could have all the money to himself. Sad to say this young man soon thought of a plan to poison his companions.

He came to the town, went to the chemist and said,

"Sell me some poison if you will,
I have a lot of rats I want to kill
And there's a polecat too about my yard
That takes my chickens and it hits me hard;
But I'll get even, as is only right,
With vermin that destroy a man by night."

The chemist replied, "I have here a poison which, if any living creature takes but the smallest mouthful, less than a grain of wheat, you will see them die down at your feet."

The young fellow grabbed the box of poison and ran into a neighbouring street. There he found a man who would lend him three large bottles. He poured poison into two, kept the third separate for himself, filled them all with wine, and sauntered back to join the other two.

Well, there's no need to make a long story of it. The other two fell on him exactly as they had planned and killed him. When they had done, the first of them said, "Now for a drink before we get to work and bury this corpse." He reached for a bottle, took one with poison, and had a swig, passed it to his companion who did the same, *and so they perished both.*

Storytelling or Drama

Retell or act out the story

The characters you need are:
  The three young men
  The boy in the pub
  The old man
  The chemist

You could split it into these scenes:

1 The drunks in the pub.
   They hear the handbell, get angry about the loss of their friend and decide to do something about Death.
2 Meeting with the old man.
   They are rude to him, threaten him. He tells them where to find Death.
3 The three of them find the money and decide what to do with it.
4 The two at the tree plan to keep the money for themselves.
5 The third goes to town and plots against the others.
6 The final killings.

Hold your own class storytelling competition
Look at pages 4, 5 and 13 for ideas for your stories.

Here is another of the stories from the "*Canterbury Tales*", told by a priest who travels with the Nun, so it's known as:

The Nun's Priest's Tale . . .

Once upon a time, long ago, a poor widow lived in a small cottage. She had lost her husband, since when she had lived a very patient, simple life, for she had very little money. She made do as best she could for herself and her three daughters, with three hefty sows, three cows, and a sheep called Molly.

She had a yard outside the cottage enclosed by a fence and surrounded by a ditch. In the yard she kept a cock called Chanticleer. He seemed a magnificent cockerel. He was the greatest of all at crowing; his voice was jollier than the organ playing in church and more regular than the abbey clock. His comb was a fine red, his bill as black as jet, his feathers bright flaming gold, his legs and toes an azure blue, with brilliant lily-white nails.

He was the master of seven hens, the loveliest of whom was gracious Lady Pertelote. Such a joy it was to hear them sing together, for in those days all animals could speak and sing.

Now it so happened that one day, just before dawn, when Chanticleer and Pertelote and all the hens were sleeping on their perches, Chanticleer began to groan and reel, so that Pertelote was quite afraid.

"What's the matter, my dear? My, what a noise to make."

"Madam," he replied, "please excuse me but I have had such a frightful dream that my heart is still pounding. I dreamt that I saw, in our yard, roaming up and down, a kind of beast, a kind of hound, which tried to sieze me and kill me. His

coat was a yellowy red, except for the tips of his ears and tail which were dark black. He had a pointed nose and glowing bright eyes. No wonder I was groaning, it was enough to make one die with fright!"

"Shame on you!" said Lady Pertelote, "You frightful coward! I cannot love you any more! We women want husbands who are tough and dependable, not men reduced to terror by a dream. Anybody with any sense knows that dreams mean nothing at all. You probably ate too much before you went to sleep. All you need is a laxative. It's no good you saying that this town doesn't have a chemist's shop. I shall prescribe you a cure from the herbs in our yard. First you'll have to eat worms for a day or two, and then, let me see, I shall find you some centaury, some fumitory, and some caper-spurge with just a touch of hellebore, and after that there's laurel, blackthorn berry and ground-ivy. They'll soon put an end to your dreams!"

"Madam, thank-you for all your advice, but I must disagree with you. Dreams often do have a meaning. I once heard a story, and I have good reason to believe it to be true, of two friends who set off on pilgrimage, but when they reached the town which was their destination, there was such a crowd of people, that they could not find anywhere to stay together. So very unwillingly they separated. The first could only find a cowshed in an innkeeper's yard to stay in, but the second was more lucky.

"Now long before daylight, this second fellow had a dream, in which his friend appeared to him and shouted. 'Help! Help! I shall be murdered tonight unless you come and help me. Come quickly!' The terrified dreamer woke up, but as soon as he realised it was a dream, he paid no attention to it and went back to sleep. Soon afterwards he had the same dream again, but again he paid no attention to it. The third time the dream was different, for this time his friend said: 'Look, I have been killed, look at my deep and bleeding wounds. You must get up, go to the west gate and there you shall see a cart loaded up with dung. Stop that cart, and hidden in the dung you shall find my body. It was for my money that they killed me.'

"The dreamer still didn't believe any of this, but he went as early as he could to where his friend had spent the night. There was no sign of him. At that moment the innkeeper arrived and said, 'Sir, your friend has gone, he left the town a little after dawn.' The man now began to feel suspicious and, drawn by the memory of the dream, off he went to the west gate. There he found a dung-cart, and the man, amazed, began to shout: 'My friend's been murdered! Fetch the sheriff! Help! My friend is killed!' People rushed out to see what the matter was, pushed the cart off its wheels, and in the middle of the dung, found the murdered man. The town officers siezed the carter and put him and the innkeeper on the rack, where both confessed. Then they took the wrecks of the bodies and hanged them both by their necks.

"So you see, Madam Pertelote, murder will always be found out, murder will out, thank God, and these stories, and many others I can think of, should teach us not to be careless about dreams. It seems to me that my dream means that something terrible will happen soon and your laxative will do me no good. But Madam, let's stop all this talk of disaster. For when I see the beauty of your face and the scarlet loveliness of your eyes, then all thoughts of terror are over. I defy all dreams and visions!"

Now it was day and with a cockle-doodle-do he flew down to the ground for he had seen a seed. He was afraid no more, but strode up and down, proud as a prince, his manly face as grim as a lion's.

All this happened in the month of March. On the third day of the May following, a sly old fox, who had been lurking round the yard for three long years, sneaked into the bed of cabbages and waited there until the middle of the day, waiting for his chance to strike. Lady Pertelote was leisurely taking a bath in the dust, surrounded by ladies basking in the sun. Chanticleer was singing merrily. And then it happened that he cast his eye towards the cabbages and saw the fox there lying low. "Cok Cok," he cried with a start and turned to fly in terror. The crafty old fox quickly said:

"Sir, wait, why do you run away? I am your friend. Surely you do not think I am waiting here to do you any harm! No sir, truly, all I wanted was to sit here and hear you sing. Such a voice you have sir, and what musical knowledge! I knew your mother. She came to my house once. But when it comes to singing — there was never anybody I would rather hear than your dear father. What pains he took — the eyes tight shut in concentration, oh — and that slender neck stretched out, that delicate beak. Oh sir, could you not, just for me, try to imitate your father?"

Poor Chanticleer was completely taken in by this flattery. He stood high upon his toes, stretched out his neck, his eyes began to close, his beak to open, and then with eyes tight shut, he began to sing.

Sir Fox then leapt to the attack, grabbed him by the neck, flung him over his back, and carried him off to the woods.

Then Dame Pertelote, and all the hens, when they saw the capture of Chanticleer set up such a yelling and shrieking that the good widow and her daughters heard all the hullabaloo, and rushing to the door saw the fox making off with Chanticleer stretched flat upon his back.

"Look," they cried, "the fox, the fox!"

Off they chased after him, with Coll the dog, and Talbot, Garland, and Moll with a distaff in her hand, in hot pursuit. The cow and calf, and even the pigs ran shouting like the fiends in hell as though their hearts would burst. The ducks left the water, squawked and flapped as though they were being slaughtered, the geese flew away in terror and the bees came out chasing out of their hive.

Now Chanticleer, though scared out of his wits, managed to blurt out, "Sir Fox, if I were you, I would turn round to these fools and shout, 'You country bumpkins you, now that I have reached the wood, you cannot catch me. I'll eat the cock at my leisure.'

The fox replied, "Good idea, it shall be done." But as he opened his mouth to speak, the nimble bird flew high into the treetops.

When the fox saw where Chanticleer had got to, he cried! "Chanticleer, I'm sorry if I have done you any harm, I didn't mean to grab you so hard. I hope I didn't frighten you. Come down sir, and I'll explain the meaning of it all."

"No sir," replied the cock. "I'm not such a dunce as all that. You won't fool me again."

So the priest ended his tale, urging his listeners to learn what truth they could from his story.

Thinking about the story

What "truth", or "moral" or "message" do you think we should find in this story? How does the writer make the meaning come across?

Decide some answers to these questions by thinking about the characters in the story.

Chanticleer

1 List all the things about Chanticleer the writer tells you which make him seem an *ordinary* cockerel, and then list all the things which make him seem *extraordinary*.
2 Answer these other questions about Chanticleer:
   What is his first reaction to his dream?
   What are his views on the meaning of dreams?
   What notice does he take of his own dream? Why?
   Why is the fox able to trick him?
   What does he think he has learned from what happens?
3 What do you think the character of Chanticleer tells us about the meaning of the story?

Pertelote

1 List all the things about Pertelote the writer tells us which make her seem an *ordinary* hen, and then list all the things which make her seem *extraordinary*.
2 Answer these questions about Pertelote:
   What does she think of Chanticleer when he is frightened by his dream?
   What are her views on the meaning of dreams?
   What is her cure for bad dreams?
   How does Pertelote like to spend her time?
3 What do you think the character of Pertelote tells us about the meaning of the story?

The Widow

1 What sort of life does the widow lead?
2 What sort of character does she have, do you think?
3 Why does the writer mention her in the story? What do you think the character of the widow tells us about the meaning of the story?

Now what are your answers to the first two questions about this story?

A Story with a Moral

The storyteller wanted to poke fun at a vain, proud character who nearly came to a sticky end because of his weaknesses. The storyteller made fun of him by showing him as a foolish cockerel, who thought himself absolutely wonderful, but who was really only an ordinary animal giving himself airs and graces in a poor widow's yard. He doesn't even take any notice when he is given warning of what is going to happen in a dream.

Try writing your own story like this — a story in which you poke fun at somebody by writing about them as an animal.

Planning

Before you start writing, you need to decide all these things:

Decide on:

1 A character that you'd like to make fun of. Somebody like:

a Boaster	a Selfish So and So
a Bully	a Tell-Tale
a Meanie	a Trickster

2 The very ordinary animal which suits this character. For example, what animal suits a boaster?
   A pig?
   A poodle?
   A tom cat?
3 What sticky end the animal might come to. Try and make it something that the animal gets into because of its weakness. Will it really happen or will it be saved?
4 The setting — where will your story take place?
5 The family and friends of the animal. Give the names and characters.
6 Does the animal get any warning of the disaster?
7 Who will be the storyteller — you? the animal? one of the animal's friends? another character?
8 How will you describe the animal? You need to try and contrast the animal's ordinary appearance and its appearance as a Boaster, or Bully or whatever you have chosen.

Drafting, revising, proofreading and presentation.

Turn to pages 14 to 17 to remind yourself about these.

Other things to do

Chaucer's English

When Geoffrey Chaucer wrote "*The Canterbury Tales*" the language, English, looked and sounded a great deal different from the language we speak and write today. First look at this page from a manuscript (a handwritten) book of "*The Pardoner's Tale*". Below it is a modern printing and a modern translation. Compare the three very carefully.

'Now, sires,' quod he, 'if that yow be so leef
To finde Deeth, turne up this croked wey,
For in that grove I lafte him, by my fey,
Under a tree, and there he wole abide;
Noght for youre boost he wole him no thing hide.
Se ye that ook? Right there ye shal him finde.
God save yow, that boghte again mankinde,
And yow amende.' Thus seyde this olde man;
And everich of thise riotoures ran
Til he cam to that tree, and ther they founde
Of florins fine of gold ycoined rounde
Wel ny an eighte busshels, as hem thoughte.

'Well, gentlemen,' said he, 'if you're so keen
To find out Death, turn up this winding road,
For on my word I left him in that grove
Under a tree, and there he will abide.
For all your braggadocio he'll not hide.
See that oak there? Right underneath you'll find
Death. God be with you, Who redeemed mankind,
And save you and amend!' said the old man.
And thereupon all three began to run
Until they reached the tree, and there they found
Gold florins, newly minted, fine and round,
And near eight bushels of them, so they thought.

1 Look at the handwritten version carefully. Which letters of the alphabet are written differently from the way we would write them today?

2 Make a list of the words which are different in Chaucer's English. Include the words which are just spelt differently and those which are very different.

3 Arrange your list in alphabetical order. Put the modern word next to it. You'll have to work out the meaning of some of the words from your modern translation.

4 Look at the opening words of "*The Canterbury Tales*" on page 80, and add any new Chaucer words to your dictionary.

The Miller

Here is part of Chaucer's description of another of his pilgrims, the Miller.

> The Millere was a stout carl for the nones;
> Ful byg he was of brawn, and eek of bones.
> That proved wel, for over al ther he cam,
> At wrastlynge he wolde have alwey the ram.
>
> 5 He was short-sholdred, brood, a thikke
>   knarre;
> Ther was no dore that he nolde heve of
>   harre,
> Or breke it at a rennyng with his head.
> His berd as any sowe or fox was reed,
> And therto brood, as though it were a spade.
>
> 10 Upon the cop right of his nose he hade
> A werte, and theron stood a toft of herys,
> Reed as the brustles of a sowes erys;
> His nosethirles blake were and wyde.
> A swerd bokeler bar be by his syde.
>
> 15 His mouth as greet was as a greet forneys.
> A baggerpipe wel koude he blowe and
>   swone,
> And therwithal he broughte us out of towne.

Have a go at putting it into modern English.
Concentrate first on the bits you can do, and have a good guess at the others. (When you've had a try, there's a modern version on page 95).

Add any new words to your dictionary of Chaucer's English.

Decorated Letters

Manuscript books were full of decorations in the capitals and between the lines. Often there were illustrations to bring out the meaning of the text. Take a short piece of writing that you have done for this unit and present it like a page from an old manuscript book.

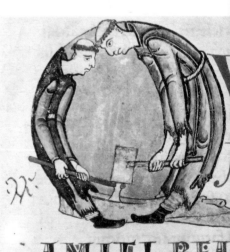

oblationes et holocausta tunc im-
ponent super altare tuum uitulos

uid gloriaris in malicia qui potes
es in iquitate.

agitur · ut in eius quoq; increpatio
ne dila__bant; ad quã tam increpa
tione quasi sub quadã reuerentia
descendunt; Unde sophar subiecit
dicens; Doctrinã qua me arguis
audiam ·& sps intelligentie mee
respondebit michi; Ac si apte dicat;
Tua quidẽ uerba audio, sed an re
cte plata sint · spũ mee intelligen
tie discerno; Nam qui docentis uer
ba despiciunt; doctrinã eius non
ad adiutoriũ sed ad occasionẽ cer
taminis sumunt; ut audita potui
iudicent quã sequant; His itaq; sub
quodã moderamine pmissis; in apta
iã beati uiri exploratione psilit

The Miller

The Miller was a big chap by the by,
A great stout fellow big in brawn and bone.
He used them very well, for he could go
And win the prize at any wrestling show.
5 Broad, knotty and short-shouldered, he
    would boast
He could heave any door off hinge and post,
Or take a run and break it with his head.
His beard, like any sow or fox, was red
And broad as well, as though it were a
    spade;
10 And, at its very tip, his nose displayed
A wart on which there stood a tuft of hair
Red as the bristles in an old sow's ear.
His nostrils were as black as they were wide.
He had a sword and buckler by his side,
15 His mighty mouth was like a furnace door.
He liked to play the bagpipes up and down
And that was how he brought us out of
town.

For the teacher

Introduction

Stories, the first chapter, introduces the method of working: reading, discussion and ideas-gathering activities, leading to the pupil's own writing. Pupils are then led briefly through the stages of planning, drafting, revising, proofreading and presentation of a finished piece of writing.

Reference Section

These pages are designed so that pupils can refer to them over the year.

The Stages of Writing illustrates the drafting and redrafting process and gives pupils a clear, step-by-step reminder of what to do at each stage.

Getting it Right offers a series of short lessons on paragraphing, punctuation and layout, which the teacher can use according to the needs of the class or of individual pupils during the year, either as introductory lessons, or as reminders.

Themes and Stories

Although arranged in a sequence, these sections could be used in any order over the year. Each *theme* consists of: a variety of reading material; written and discussion work; language study; and sometimes drama, leading to a major piece of writing, or a collection of writing on a related topic, as shown in the chart.

The three *stories* are designed to develop children's response to a varied selection of narratives. The essential feature of these chapters will be a vivid presentation of the story. Teachers will want to read much more of this material to the class. Each story is presented in parts. Pairs or groups could then tackle the reading themselves. Pupils are asked to review their understanding of what they have read and to consider what they expect to happen next.

Using the material

Much of the material has been in use for several years with mixed-ability, multi-ethnic classes. Although suitable for any class, the material works well with mixed-ability classes for the following reasons:

1 There is a mixture of material to be read, discussed and worked over with the whole class; common pieces of writing with scope for pupils to choose treatment and style; and sections from which teacher and pupils can choose activities. At the end of each theme or story, there is a section called *Other things to do*. There is work here for fast finishers of all abilities, with room for choice.

2 There is a range of reading material, varied in both length and difficulty. More difficult reading material can be used with the whole class if it is prepared and read aloud by the teacher. Longer pieces could be tackled in pairs or groups. The division into manageable chunks with questions for discussion helps pupils work together to review their understanding of what they have read.

3 Working regularly through the *Stages of Writing,* with the help of the Reference Section, encourages collaboration as pupils read each other's work, and leads to valuable pupil discussion. Accuracy is developed by revising and proofreading one's own writing, rather than by isolated exercises taken out of context. The emphasis on presentation helps children of all abilities take a pride and see a value in their writing, however modest.

4 The Reference Section helps pupils to work at their own pace, independently of the teacher.

5 Questions are not intended to be worked through unselectively by pupils working alone. They can be used selectively with the whole class, orally as a check on understanding with pairs or groups, or as individual writing tasks, according to the teacher's judgement of the class's needs and the pace of the lessons.

Chapter	Reading	Oral work	Main writing tasks
Stories	Biography, stories	Retelling stories, drama. Prediction, and discussion	Story The Stages of Writing
Creation	Poem, description, stories	Discussion — comparing two stories	Description Planning
The Story of Sun and Moon	Story	Discussion of response to the story	Story Making a collection of different kinds of writing
Animals	Poems	Reading and taping poems Discussion — opinion	Poems Opinion
Stories from the Ramayana	Stories	Drama	Writing about characters Making notes Making a display of writing
The Story of Harriet Tubman	Biography	Drama	Making and using notes Collecting vocabulary Playwriting
Fears and Superstitions	Poems, stories, biography, pupils' writing	Discussion — personal experiences	A collection of writing on a theme — personal, poetry and story Collecting vocabulary
The Canterbury Tales	Description, stories, pupils' writing	Discussion — character and response to a story	Analysing characters Description A story with a moral Language study